YOU CAN BE EMOTIONALLY HEALED

MORRIS SHEATS

Copyright © 1994 by Leadership Institute. All rights reserved. No part of this book may be reproduced or transmitted in any form or by any means, electronic or mechanical, including photocopying, recording, or by any information storage and retrieval system, without the written permission from the Publisher.

Published By: Christian Life Publications, P. O. Box 8786, Columbus, GA 31908-8786.

Unless otherwise stated, all Bible quotations are taken from the King James Translation.

THE LIVING BIBLE, Copyright 1971 Tyndale House Publishers, used by permission

CONTENTS

Chapter 1	You Can Be Emotionally Healed	1
Chapter 2	The Healing of the Memories	13
Chapter 3	Wounded Hearts	25
Chapter 4	Broken Dreams	37
Chapter 5	The Hidden Child Within You	49
Chapter 6	Spiritual Answers to Financial Problems	61
Chapter 7	Reactions	73
Chapter 8	How to Turn Sorrow Into Joy	83
Chapter 9	Suffering: The Common Denominator	95
Chapter 10	How to Handle Fear	107
Chapter 11	The Danger of Comparison	119
Chapter 12	Causes of Depression	131
Chapter 13	How to Receive the Greatest Benefit from Your Problems	145
Afterword	Keeping Your Emotional Healing	159

PUBLISHER'S FOREWORD TO THE FIRST EDITION

You are about to embark upon a reading experience that will change your life. The following pages contain some of the most needed teaching and biblically sound advice that we have read. At some time or another, you will probably experience one or more of the emotional problems which Morris Sheats has dealt with so effectively. With this in mind, we have provided blank pages at the end of each chapter for personal notes. When you read something that applies to you or someone you know, make a note of it. When the Holy Spirit reveals to you an area of your life that needs changing, make a note of it. Don't count on your memory to record it.

We are humbled to have been chosen to publish this fine book and pray that it will help you, and others through you, in the days to come.

CHAPTER 1

YOU CAN BE EMOTIONALLY HEALED

God wants us to be whole! And we can be whole, for God's grace is sufficient; it is more than enough to keep us strong no matter what happens.

As we read in Job 22:21, we are given a provocative statement: "Acquaint now thyself with him, and be at peace..." This is a tremendous promise. It says plainly that the way to peace and goodness is to acquaint yourself with God.

You cannot really, honestly acquaint yourself with God without finding peace. The world is searching to find peace today. We are very familiar with our problems - we give them first place in our thinking. We want to be free from them and live at peace.

Not long ago a man said to me, "Before long, I'm going to get a raise and our financial problems are going to be over. We're finally going to live in peace." I looked at that man and said, "Have you really given yourself to God?" "Oh, not completely," he said. Then I spoke these words: "I don't mean to be rude or harsh with you, but that raise you are anticipating will not bring the peace you are expecting. Peace begins inside - it is not external." When we know God; when we acquaint ourselves with Him; then, and only then, do we begin to know peace.

Of course, finding peace means freedom from guilt. It means freedom from all memories of the past. The more you acquaint yourself with God, the more He heals your memories. The result will be a deep and abiding peace. (Chapter Two)

Job 22:21 goes on to say, "Good shall come unto thee." You see, a promise of God is to bring good to His children. I wish, once and for all, that we could destroy the Puritan idea that God is mean and nasty, wanting to send you into the pits of hell. Do not misunderstand me, there is a day of Judgment. There will be a time when men will face eternal destiny. But I know in my heart, and according to the Bible, that God wants the very best for all His children. I'm convinced that He wants good to come into your households. So acquaint yourselves with God and then good shall come unto you. You can quit worrying about what tomorrow will bring because, as the Apostle Paul points out, if you love God, everything will eventually work out for good.

I have a little sign in my study which I read every day. It says, "Today is the tomorrow you worried about yesterday." There's a great deal of truth in that statement. We are constantly worrying about what's going to happen tomorrow. A major step toward emotional healing is to understand that God wants good to come your way.

You might say then, "Why is it that I always have setbacks? Why is it, then, that I do not always have good coming in my direction?" It is because we live in a world where there are forces of good and forces of evil, and from time to time we will face exposure to the forces of evil. But it is not God's desire that we live constantly under the bondage of satan. It is His desire that we be set free and live in a state of goodness.

Even today as I write, God's goodness is present. I look over a very peaceful English countryside. The brook is bubbling. the sheep are resting - "even in green pastures." I am here with my wife resting. It is only by God's goodness.

Having just returned from teaching national pastors in Kumasi, Ghana, I am acutely aware of my present surroundings and those conditions a few days ago.

In Kumasi the accommodations were sparse but adequate. No hot water most of the time. Often no electricity, yet I experienced the goodness of God there as much as here in this lovely English countryside where there is abundance. God is good and desires to shower His goodness on us.

Our problem is that we do not believe that our Heavenly Father wants to provide His goodness to us. We concentrate on our weaknesses rather than His strengths. The result is often a sense of defeat rather than an experiencing of God's goodness.

Often these defeats and setbacks leave us with a wounded heart. We are like the man on the road to Jericho - robbed, wounded, and left to die! But remember, God is the healer of wounded hearts, and good shall come unto you. (Chapter Three)

Job 22:22 reads: "Receive, I pray thee, the law from his mouth, and lay up his words in thine heart." This is a powerful step to emotional healing. When you keep God's Words in your mouth and lay up His Words in your heart, you will have emotional stability. Meditating on God's Words brings great strength.

When you dream a dream and find it hasn't worked out, what do you do? Do you give up and quit? The best procedure is to meditate upon the Word of God. As you do this God will enable you to live through that broken dream.

In 1987 I experienced a devastating defeat in my professional life. I was asked to pioneer a new church in North Dallas. There were only a few families involved and I was forty-four years old.

Having helped pioneer the Trinity Church in Lubbock, Texas, I knew the price to be paid to start any congregation. I had seen the Trinity Church grow to be one of America's largest interdenominational churches. It continues to flourish abundantly long after I have left.

The fulfillment of creating, with God's help, a flourishing congregation is a supreme joy. Yet, the pain of testing in the birthing years can be almost overwhelming to one's mental, physical, and spiritual capacities.

So, only after much prayer with my family, was the decision made to begin, with a few families, the dream of Hillcrest Church in North Dallas.

When severe governmental problems arose only two and one-half years into the building of the dream, I was devastated. It was only prayer, the loyalty of my family, the prayers of others, and the intense meditation of God's Word that sustained me. You can live through broken dreams and dream again. (Chapter Four)

Job 22:23 says: "If thou return to the Almighty, thou shalt be built up..." Most doctors will tell you that between sixty and eighty percent of our illnesses are caused by nervous disorders. They are illnesses caused by constant worry about tomorrow.

But God is saying to us, "I want to build you up. I want to strengthen you." What does He mean by that? Read what Paul says in I Corinthians 14. "When someone speaks in a tongue, when someone prophesies, when someone gives a special message, let it build up the body of Christ." There is hope and we can be built up in God.

Part of the process of being built up in God is being liberated from the hidden child within you. All people have a child that still seems to cause problems even though they may be an adult. The child that was hurt or wounded still seems to control the adult. That hidden child within you may be the source of many physical and emotional problems.

Fortunately, when you are built up in God you can also be set free from the hidden child within you.

Most of us have a struggle with the child within as adults. I did and, perhaps at times, still do. However, a remarkable healing occurred when I was forty-seven years of age. I faced the truth.

My parents were wonderful in many ways. Having been the products of the Great Depression, they worked hard to overcome poverty. My father had a dramatic spiritual conversion in his early thirties. He left "dirt farming" (I never quite understood the term…what else would you call it?) and entered the ministry of the church.

The church he entered was very legalistic. Everything about life was "bad or evil." I now realize that early in my life I subconsciously rejected that lifestyle. I determined to be positive.

The child within, however, always haunted me. If I was successful and reached a dream, I felt guilty. It was the child within who had been taught well the "do not's of life" and not the "do's of life."

At forty-seven, I realized my parents did the best they knew. They provided well. They loved me. They even sacrificed to provide travel. It was the "religious system" that controlled their minds and emotions and thus was passed on to me.

Finally, thanks be to God, I learned God's grace and mercy could heal the child within. (Chapter Five)

The next step to emotional healing has to do with money. If there's any one thing that people are worried about today it's the economy of the American system. We are in a worldwide recession. People are concerned. It's the number one topic of conversation. The economic status of the land is more dominant in the minds of people than politics or the weather. People are not sure what will happen to the value of gold and silver. But when we begin to put ourselves in the right relationship with God, He will take care of us no matter what happens. Emotional healing can only take place when you turn your finances over to God.

Many people can turn everything over to God except their money. They can relinquish everything except their business - and then they begin holding on like a dying man clinging to a two-by-four in the middle of the ocean. The only answer to our financial crises as Christians is the entire commitment of our income to God. Just say, "Father, here it is - you take it and use it."

When you pray that prayer, you are going to find some answers to the financial problem. You will find that turning your money over to God brings great freedom. After all, the government cannot give us all the answers we need to the problems of a sagging economy or rising prices. Fortunately, there are some answers. (Chapter Six)

When you live as close as possible to God's principles, you will find that He will be your strength and defense. No longer do you have to react to every situation in a negative way. No longer do you need to respond defensively to each situation of life. When you begin to learn that God is your defense, then you can learn the importance of positive reactions.

I remember at forty-seven years of age my father saying to me, "You better be careful, you are very successful and you are getting too big for your pants." I had put on a few pounds, but that is not what dad meant.

"Too much success" - whatever that means - was not healthy in my father's mind. I remember that day. I decided to accept that my father's words were sincere - from his perspective. I chose to react positively and to believe that God's goodness and blessings were part of His very nature. You can do the same. (Chapter Seven)

In Job 22:26, a further message is given: "Then thou shalt have thy delight…(Delight means joyful satisfaction.)…for then thou shalt have thy delight in the Almighty and shalt lift up thy face unto God." In other words, as you acquaint yourself with God, as you are edified and built up, as you realize that God is taking care of your finances, then you are going to have delight in Him.

Now, I know a lot of Christians who love the Lord but have no satisfaction in God. They have lost the joy. They have lost the bubble. They have lost the fizz. It's all gone. Life is a drag. They've got to go to church. It's another obligation, it's another duty - it's something they must do.

When you begin to be really emotionally healed, you will realize that God is taking care of you and yours. He is building you up. He is bringing good things into your storehouse. The result is that you are going to have some sheer satisfaction, some pure joy, some glorious happiness way down deep inside that says you do not have to be frustrated or defeated anymore.

I know that satan comes to every believer and tries to bring depression and frustration. But the Bible says in the book of Romans that, "We are more than conquerors through Christ Jesus who has strengthened us." I have counseled with many people in the last few months who have had problems of frustration, problems of anxiety. I have seen them healed by the power of God. How did this happen? By realizing that God is on the throne. When one realizes that life is eternal, then a lot of things we place importance on today become unimportant.

I remember speaking in a class at Texas Tech University a few years ago. After class a very inquisitive young man began to press me about a number of things I had said. Since that time, I have seen him grow in spiritual understanding and knowledge because he was reaching out for more of God. In a conversation we had later, he said something like this: "Pastor, wouldn't it be great if we could all go to the park some Sunday and just praise the Lord all day long?" I have never forgotten that. There are times in my heart when that is exactly what I want to do. I get tired of schedules. I want to go to a place where I can just close myself in and not worry about time. I want to delight in the presence of God. And that is the kind of emotional healing that God wants to bring, a healing of sheer delight.

When you begin to experience the true emotional healing that God brings, you will even experience that God can turn your sorrows into joy. You may have many heartaches. You may have many disappointments. However, it is so exciting to know that part of the emotional healing is the hand of God touching your life and allowing you to experience joy instead of sorrow. (Chapter Eight)

I especially receive a blessing from Job 22:27: "Thou shalt make thy prayer unto him, and he shall hear thee..." It is truly exciting to know that God hears your prayers. You might be saying, "Well, He has not answered my prayer." Yes, God answers all of our prayers. He may say "Yes" or "No" or "Wait awhile." But He does give us an answer.

Our problem is that so often we are not willing to accept His answer. Suffering comes our way and we feel that God has forgotten us. It is easy to forget that suffering is the common denominator of all humanity. Even when you are suffering, you can reach out to God in prayer and He does hear you.

My wife, Janet, has battled Multiple Sclerosis for fifteen years. She has suffered at times immensely. At other times healing by God's hand seems to be more apparent. I do not mean the ebb and flow of the disease; I mean the times of release and the times of torment caused by the disease.

At times her suffering is so intense - both physically and emotionally - that I do not know what to do to try to help. At those times, I pray even more.

Often in a week's time, I go to the House of Prayer at our church and seek God in my wife's behalf. Prayer brings relief in my heart. Often the outward conditions seem to remain, but the inner man is strengthened.

Is that not what the Apostle Paul declared? "The outer man perishes, but the inward man is renewed day by day." God hears us when we pray and chooses in His own special way to help us - even in times of suffering. (Chapter Nine)

I was watching a group of eighth-graders being interviewed on the news recently. Each was saying something like this: "I always thought we could believe in our government, but now, I don't know who to believe." We are living in an age when even our children are aware that we cannot be sure what is true and what is false. I plead with you to understand one thing clearly: when you do not know whether to believe what you are hearing today from the news media or your own friends and neighbors, I can assure you that everything decreed in the infallible Word of God is established; it is true and you can bank your very life on it.

When God's Word really becomes a part of your inner life, you have something upon which to base your life. No longer can fear beat you into the ground when a problem arises. You have confidence because of God's Word.

The enemy of your soul is fear. When you think about the negative things of the world, you will become a negative person full of fear. Conversely, when you think about the positive things of God you can become a strong person - able to handle any fear that comes to you. (Chapter Ten)

When a person needs emotional healing, it's like being in a room that's barely lit. He is still functioning, he can still maneuver through life, but when a person needs emotional healing, a haze hovers over his soul and he cannot see the light.

You may not even know that the light has grown dim in your soul. But when Jesus walks in and you acquaint yourself with God, then you begin to receive His peace. The light comes in. You no longer walk in the hazy fog of darkness; you walk in the abundant light of God.

I have talked with many people who struggled in the darkness of emotional instability. They were looking for light. I have seen it happen to hundreds of people; when God's light would shine upon their way they would begin to accept themselves and not try to continue comparing themselves with everyone else. As long as you compare yourself with others, the chances are that you will not be emotionally whole. God has asked you to be happy with the person you are; to accept yourself. When you do that you are free from the sin of comparison. (Chapter Eleven)

Job 22:29 says: "When men are cast down, then thou shalt say, there is lifting up…" When you are cast down, there is lifting up. I think that we live in the most cast-down age that the world has ever known. The sale of tranquilizers has become a multi-million dollar business. People are trying to find an answer to their problems in a pill. I am not chiding you if you're on some kind of medication. I am for doctors; I am for scientific research. But I want to make it clear that the Lord desires to bring us to the place where we can be so acquainted with Him that we will have peace when there is no peace around us.

God wants to teach us that when men are cast down (or, if we put that in modern vernacular, when men are really depressed) when they are weighted beneath the anxieties of life, then there is a lifting up. And where does that lifting up come from? When you acquaint yourself with God, He comes in and He lifts you up with His own hands. He undergirds you; He strengthens you. No matter what comes your way, He strengthens you.

A lady was walking across the park late at night. She had been working late, and on her way home a man began to pursue her. When she increased her pace, he increased his pace. Finally, he came very close to her. She was frightened and she did not know what to say, but she thought of a verse in Psalms which says that His presence covers us with feathers like the mother hen. She turned around and screamed very loudly, "I'm covered with feathers! I'm covered with feathers!"

The man immediately changed directions with great speed. You see, God wants you to know you are covered. He wants you to know that no matter what happens to you, you are alright!

I am convinced that when depression sets in (depression being part of emotional destruction) people fail to remember the Word of God. In fact, I am going to say it exactly as I believe it: If satan can take up your time so that you do not have time to really stay in the Word of God, I can promise you, you are headed for emotional problems. A man or woman cannot function today in the pressurized container known as the world without falling, unless he or she is renewed in the inner spirit daily.

Why do you think the suicide rate is rising every year among teens and college students? They feel the pressure. I have counseled with a number of college students who have said, "Pastor, I don't really want to be in school. I'm just there for someone else's benefit. I have to make good grades and the pressure is overwhelming." They begin to feel claustrophobic. Do you ever feel closed in because you know you have to make a living? You have to keep going; you must keep functioning. People are depending on you. A mother said to me the other day, "If I stop, everything falls apart. They depend upon me too much in my household." And we live in this pressure cooker. Imagine it. It is like one of those pressurized deodorant cans, a potentially explosive bomb. And the only way to keep it from going off is to let the Word of God fill your heart in order to equalize the pressure. (Chapter Twelve)

There's no one on earth who will ever find an answer to his emotional problems until he humbles himself before God. So long as you believe you can solve all your problems yourself, they will never be solved. So long as you believe that you are the answer and you do not have to have God's help, you will continue to live in frustration. You say, "How can I begin?" Begin as Job 22:21 says: "...acquaint thyself with God." Then you will find peace. (Chapter Thirteen)

If you feel a little tattered around the edges, if you have wondered whether life is worth living, then get alone with God this week and re-evaluate your priorities. You may be spending time on things in which you should not be investing your life. It may be that you are exerting effort in directions that are not very beneficial. When Haggai prophesied to the people, he said, "Yes, you are living in beautiful homes. Yes, you are making lots of money; but you are putting your money into purses that have holes in them." There are times when people seem to work harder than they ever have, and all they get for it is a purse with a hole in it. This is because their priorities are not straight. So long as your priorities are incorrect, you will never experience peace. But once you establish your relationship with God as the most important, then other priorities are going to fall into proper perspective. As long as anything else takes precedence over getting acquainted with God, then you will be confused and frustrated on the inside.

God wants to do a work. He would like to reach out and help those who need emotional healing. He is saying, "I love you and I want to make you well." Begin to get acquainted with God and you will have His peace, and that peace will bring you spiritual and physical prosperity. Remember the powerful principle in the New Testament:

"Allow God's peace to be the ruler (literally - umpire) in your heart."

Colossians 3

CHAPTER 2

THE HEALING OF THE MEMORIES

Is any sick among you? Let him call for the elders of the church; and let them pray over him, anointing him with oil in the name of the Lord: And the prayer of faith shall save the sick, and the Lord shall raise him up: and if he hath committed sins, they shall be forgiven him. Confess your faults one to another, and pray one for another, that ye may be healed. The effectual fervent prayer of a righteous man availeth much.

James 5:14-16

When we talk about the matter of emotional healing, we have to deal with people's concept of God. For our concept of God is almost always related to our concept of our parents. That's the way God intended it to be, for He established the home before He ever established the church. So what is your concept of God? Perhaps He is an Old Testament God. Stern. Never bending. Always ready to knock you on the head when you step out of line.

A person said to me once, "My dad was always right. He was 'never wrong' in the nineteen years I was home, and I guess God is the same way. How could God possibly understand my problems?"

Some people have what I call a Runaway God. They believe there is a God somewhere, but they are afraid He will not hear them if they call on Him. As one young person said during counseling, "My dad ran away when I was little. I've always been afraid of God. I'm afraid He won't be there when I need Him, just like my dad was never there when I needed him."

Then there is the Santa Claus God. One young adult said to me, "My parents always gave me things, things, things, but they never really cared about me. They were like Santa Claus, not entirely real. I'm afraid God will be that way."

Then there are many people who have a concept of God as a good God because their parents were good. Their parents tried to do what was right. Their parents strived to be fair. Their parents tried to be kind rather than harsh although they were firm when necessary. If a child has a good set of parents, they usually have a good concept of God.

We come now to a very solemn point in this writing. We must be cleansed from all misconceptions of God. We must be cleansed from all of our hidden sins and our hidden images of who God is. I have said to many people in counseling, "If my God were the kind of God you describe, I would not serve Him either." Their idea of God was completely wrong.

> *Who can understand his errors? (or as one translation has it, "hidden sins") Cleanse thou me from secret faults. Keep back thy servant also from presumptuous sins; let them not have dominion over me, then shall I be upright and I shall be innocent from the great transgression.*
>
> Psalm 19:12-13

The psalmist, David, is asking God to keep him from those hidden sins.

We must also deal honestly with our problems. More than ever before as a pastor I am realizing how important it is that we meet the problems of others with utter honesty. If we do not, then we force people to be dishonest. There is a very subtle line that has to be drawn here in the Christian walk. Of all the people in the world, Christians are to have the most hope and joy. But, by the same token, we have to understand that there are times of disappointment, shattered dreams, times of broken hopes. And to be dishonest about these times, to say that they do not exist, is to be untruthful.

As a result, when we force people to be dishonest, they put up a veneer. They look right, they walk right, they dress right, say the right thing, answer the questions with the right answers. Yet, down deep inside they are aching and torn apart because they have not been allowed to be honest and to say, "Yes, I have a problem." As a pastor, I have seen the veneer hundreds of times. So let us consider how to get past the veneer to the real person inside of you.

I. GOD IS THE KIND OF GOD YOU CAN LOVE.

First, I want you to know that GOD IS THE KIND OF GOD THAT YOU CAN LOVE. He is a God filled with concern. He wants you to be whole and free from defeat. He does not want to punish you. There is going to be a time of judgment. There is an eternal heaven and hell. However, hell is the last place God wants you to be. He wants you in heaven. He gave His only Son so that you could find eternal life. God does not want to beat you down over something you did six days or six weeks or six years ago. God want you to be set free. That is why the Bible says:

> *There is therefore now no condemnation to them wich are in Christ Jesus, who walk not after the flesh, but after the Spirit.*
>
> Romans 8:1

As long as you are walking after Christ, as long as you are trying to walk in the Spirit, you have no reason to bow down to self-condemnation and guilt whether you feel like it or not. God wants you free from all condemnation because God is the kind of God you can love. I want to tell you how to be set free from condemnation of the past.

II. THE MEMORY

You have a memory inside of you. You have something that makes you calculate what has happened during all the moments of your life. It is logged together like a giant computer within your brain. I have read articles stating if we were to build a computer as effective as one person's brain, it would be ten stories high and two blocks across. Think about it! All that in a little computer that God has locked in your head.

Let's begin by considering how God made our mind. We have a conscious part of our mind. You are conscious right now as you are reading what I have written. There is another part of you that is down deep inside. Psychology calls it the subconscious. We know scientifically that our subconscious is imprinted with everything that has ever happened to us - all the good things as well as all the bad things. That is why the psalmist David said:

> *Thy word have I hid in mine heart, (in my subconscious mind in the deep part of my personality) that I might not sin against Thee.*
>
> Psalm 119:11

Let me digress long enough to say something to parents. Please teach your children Scripture verses even though they may not have complete comprehension of everything they learn. Let those little ones memorize the Word of God. Buy a box of "Precious Promises" and go through the Bible and mark those verses. Let them learn the Word of God, from the Word of God. The more of the Word a child tucks into his heart, the less chance he will have of forgetting God.

In this computer that God has placed in your head called the mind, you have imprinted all the good impressions and all of the bad ones. For example, if you get up in the morning feeling tired and deprived of sleep; if you find yourself easily irritable; if you have a tendency to withdraw or to fall into a state of depression, I would urge you to suspect experiences of the past that may still be haunting you. As a pastor, I have seen this happen in many cases.

In one particular case, a person had no problems growing up so far as materials things were concerned. All the material goods of life were supplied. In fact, they were supplied in abundance. The problem was never one of having too little, rather, discomfort lay in having too much. This individual told me, "You know, I don't feel like I was ever accepted simply as a person. I was just an object upon which to lavish gifts because it was easier to spend money than time." Here was that person later on as an adult - irritable, leaning toward withdrawal, depressed for several hours or days at a time. As we began to seek God together in this matter, we discovered that it was only when the memories were healed that this individual could be released and set free.

Now, when I speak of the healing of the memories, I am not advocating any ordinary kind of prayer. I'm not talking about, "Now I lay me down to sleep," or "Lord, heal my memories. Thank you, God. Amen." I'm talking about an intensive type of prayer, a prayer of faith that travels through the corridors of your mind picking up the pieces that have been broken.

Someone might be asking right now, "Well, Pastor Sheats, if I have this kind of prayer will I lose my memories? Will I remember what happened?" The answer is "Yes." You will continue to remember, but instead of remembering with that feeling of hurt; instead of remembering with that feeling of lust; instead of remembering with that feeling of rejection; when the healing of the memories takes place by the divine scalpel of the Holy Spirit, you may remember the incidents, but you will not remember the pain.

How does it work? Primarily, in two steps.

1. Remember that Jesus Christ transcends all time.

The Bible tells us:

> *Jesus Christ is the same yesterday, today and forever.*
>
> Hebrews 13:8

> *John bare witness of him, and cried, saying, This was he of whom I spake, He that cometh after me is preferred before me; for he was before me.*
>
> John 1:15

John is saying that Jesus, who came after him, actually lived before him. And what is he talking about? He's talking about Christ Who was ordained with the Father and the Spirit even before the world began. The same thing is brought out in another passage.

> *Then said the Jews unto him, Thou art not yet fifty years old, and hast thou seen Abraham? Jesus said unto them, Verily, verily I say unto you, Before Abraham was, I am.*
>
> John 8:57, 58

In other words, before Abraham ever existed, Jesus was saying, "I exist." This is what we call the transcendence of Christ. He transcends all time. You say, "Well, why is that important?" It's important because, through prayer, Jesus can walk back through the corridors of time and actually heal your memories. If He transcends all time, He can walk back with you through all the time you have ever known and heal you.

2. There is a child within you that needs to be healed.

I find in counseling that quite often there are three types of children that still live within us as an adult. There is the hurt child, the child who was rejected by his parents, and possibly, by his peers. There is the hating child, the child who is filled with hate because he has known nothing but hatred. There is the horrified child, the child filled with fear. These three children (one or more) may show themselves in the adult.

The writings of David Seamonds first introduced me to the truth of how the child within often controls our adult lives. I am grateful.

I have come to realize, and to observe both personally and in others, that the power of Jesus Christ can heal the memories. What often takes years in psychotherapy can be accomplished through prayer. I am not suggesting that this "prayer method" is a pollyanna cure-all. There must be proper preparation of the heart to receive the healing. The process is not complicated, but it is very important.

I suggest that we allow the Holy Spirit to take you back through the corridors of your mind to times when you may have been the hurting child or the hating child or the horrified child. The Holy Spirit and the power of Jesus can transcend all time, so let Him march back through the corridors of your mind and allow Him to heal the child within.

When you come to an incident and see yourself hurting; you see yourself hating as a child; you see yourself horrified, full of fear; I want you to imagine Jesus Christ taking you up in his arms and saying, "Let the children come unto me, for of such is the kingdom of God." (Some people even find it beneficial to briefly write a description of these times.) If this truth can penetrate your heart, it will change your whole life. You do not have to be haunted; you do not have to be hurt; you do not have to be hateful. For you can say, "I am no longer defeated. Jesus Christ has taken me up in His arms, and He has said to me, 'Come unto me, for the kingdom of God is made of children.'"

I can just see Jesus taking those little children, those who have been hurt, those who were hated, those who were full of fear, wrapping his arms around them, hugging them and saying, "I love you. I love you." Every time that child comes out inside of you, stop and imagine Jesus taking you up as a child and saying, "I love you. I care deeply for you. The hurt does not have to stay there. The hating does not have to remain. Those fears and horrors do not have to live in your heart because I love you."

I must now caution you in two areas. First, do not offend children. We should never deliberately hurt a child. The Bible says:

> *But whoso shall offend one of these little ones which believe in me, it were better for him that a millstone were hanged about his neck, and that he were drowned in the depth of the sea.*
>
> Matthew 18:6

Why? Because we are influencing future adults. We are molding the men and women who will lead our church and our nation tomorrow. God warns us, as adults, not to offend children in order that they may grow up without "the child within" controlling them.

The second caution I must give you is not to get too involved in introspection. I personally believe that it is a trick of satan to try to get you involved in analysis of yourself to see how terrible you are and end up in a depressed state of mind. Once you go back through the corridors of time and allow the Holy Spirit to eradicate those hurt feelings, and those hating feelings, and those horrified feelings, simply praise the Lord. You are free of the past.

Do not keep going back through the past. It is over. It is settled. It is done. When Jesus said, "It is finished," on the cross, He was not only talking about salvation. He was saying, "Now, Father, I have done all you want me to do and my life is complete." When you come to Jesus and know Him as your Lord and as your Savior, you have the right to stand up and say, "It is finished. My old self no longer lives, but Jesus lives in me. My life is complete."

III. STEPS TO THE HEALING OF THE MEMORIES

Four important STEPS must be taken into account when we deal with THE HEALING OF THE MEMORIES.

1. Have someone to pray with you.

It is very important to have someone to pray with you. James 5:13-16 is our best guide. Call for an elder or spiritual leader to pray a prayer of faith with you for that healing. Why do I say it is important to have someone to pray with you? Because many times if you try to go through this process of praying for the healing of your past, satan can very quickly beat you down and say, "Look at you. Who do you think you are? Singing in the choir. Teaching a Sunday school class. Going to that church? Who are you, anyway?" You can be smothered by negative thoughts at that moment. However, if you have a dear believer with you - a Godly spiritual leader whom you love and trust, you can be sustained in that hour of prayer. Together you can defeat all the power of the enemy. The Word says:

> *And again I say unto you, that if two of you shall agree on earth as touching any thing that they shall ask, it shall be done for them of my Father which is in heaven.*
>
> Matthew 18:19

When you pray, pray in confidence. What do I mean by that? Exactly this. If you ask a spiritual leader to pray with you, there should be the kind of relationship between you where you would not have to worry about the spiritual leader broadcasting it to someone else. God deliver us from busybodies and gossips. The Church does not need anyone with a long tongue. We need to stand together. When a person says, "Something happened to me a long time ago and I want you to join me in prayer that I will be healed," you will say, "Yes, I will pray with you, and it will remain only between you and myself and the Father." Over the years I have absolutely refused to discuss the cases I've counseled - even with my wife. When we pray together for one another, there must be an attitude of love, deep concern, and confidence.

2. Pray conversationally.

What do I mean by that? I mean, avoid getting in a hurry. Do not say,

"Oh, God, in the next thirty seconds I want you to heal me of my memories - of all the things that should not be in my mind." Rather, take some time and pray conversationally, and as two or three pray together you can visualize Jesus comforting the child. I imagine Jesus picking up that child and saying, "Beloved, turn it over to me, for I love you." Do not be afraid. As you pray conversationally, let the Spirit fill your mind.

3. Fill your mind with God's Word.

When you are healed, what happens? You have been forgiven. I am glad that those memories that might have haunted us for years can be absolutely forgiven. I am not talking about brushing them underneath the rug and saying, "They are not there." No, that is a part of the dishonesty I wrote about in the beginning . Rather, when you face reality saying, "Yes, I experienced some things in my past that I do not like, but as I remember them, it helps me to grow spiritually. Then remembering and being healed, I no longer hurt."

Do you see how it works? You are no longer filled with anger and hate. Guilt has been taken away. Sins are washed away and joy invades the heart. God has cleared your record. When God comes down into your life and heals you of the past, your record is made completely clean. You no longer live the way you used to live. You remember, but the memory is healed.

Now, get honest with yourself. Stop living behind a facade. Stop deceiving yourself. Admit that guilt has robbed you of joy. Ask His forgiveness and receive His healing.

> *All day and all night your hand was heavy on me. My strength evaporated like water on a sunny day until I finally admitted all my sins to you and stopped trying to hide them. I said to myself, I will confess them to the Lord. And you forgave me! And my guilt is gone.*
>
> Psalm 32:4,5 (Living Bible)

As you fill your mind with God's Word, you begin to realize that new power is flowing within you. You start knowing that you are forgiven.

One of the reasons many people do not have any strength throughout the day is that they are burdened with a load of guilt. So long as they carry it around, they do not have any strength. Each sinner should confess his sins to God while he is aware of them and while there is time to be forgiven. Judgment will not touch him if he asks forgiveness.

Now take a minute and review.

Number one, have someone to pray with you. Number two' pray conversationally, picturing Jesus taking up the child in you and saying, "I love you." Number three, fill your mind with God's Word.

4. Remember that Jesus is alive, and He is in you when you receive Him.

The apostle Paul continually writes to the New Testament Christians reminding them that they are "in Christ." The old self has been destroyed. The new self comes alive. This "exchanged life" happens when you receive Jesus Christ into your life. If you have never received Jesus Christ, you can do so now. Here is a prayer to pray:

"Jesus Christ, I do believe you are the Son of God. I do believe that you came to the earth and lived, died, and rose again for me. I confess my sins to you and receive you as my Savior and Lord."

Ps 31

CHAPTER 3

WOUNDED HEARTS

And Jesus answering said, A certain man went down from Jerusalem to Jericho, and fell among thieves, which stripped him of his raiment, and wounded him and departed leaving him half dead. And by chance there came down a certain priest that way; and when he was at the place, came and looked on him and he passed by on the other side. And likewise a Levite, when he was at the place, came and looked on him, and passed by on the other side. But a certain Samaritan, as he journeyed, came where he was; and when he saw him, he had compassion on him, And went to him, and bound up his wounds, pouring in oil and wine, and set him on his own beast, and brought him to an inn, and took care of him. And on the morrow when he departed, he took out two pence, and gave them to the host, and said unto him, Take care of him; and whatsoever thou spendest more, when I come again, I will repay thee. Which now of these three thinkest thou, was a neighbor unto him that fell among the thieves? And he said, He that showed mercy on him. Then said Jesus unto him, Go, and do thou likewise.

Luke 10: 30-37

Most of the time when we have heard this passage, the emphasis has been about the good Samaritan; how a man stopped to help another man who was in trouble. This time, however, I want to talk about the man who was injured. I do not know his name; I do not know his background; the Bible does not say much about him. It does say that he was wounded. He lay by the road side. He was wounded and there he lay. This could have been any person. It could be you or it could be me, because many times in life we find ourselves wounded. Something happens to us and we are wounded. A man once told me many years ago the following story.

"I had a great deal of money. I was very successful, but due to circumstances in my life I lost not only my money, I lost my family. I lost my way and I am a defeated man." That person was wounded. On another occasion I said to a lovely young lady whom I had met for the first time, "I see that you are engaged, soon to be married, I suppose." She said, just in a whisper, "No, you see my fiance was killed just six months ago." She also had a wounded heart. A young man walked down an aisle of our church, as he took my hand with tears streaming down his face, he said, "Pastor, you know I left a few days ago on my way to California to get married?" I said, "Yes, Ron, I remember. What's wrong? Why are you on crutches and limping?" He told me that in a tragic accident his fiance was killed. Yes, he was injured physically, but more, so much more painful was the wound he suffered emotionally.

Many times I have been by the side of people in the hospital room after a doctor had just pronounced that they have no chance for survival. Sometimes they are told they will be an invalid all the days of their life. Yes, I have seen people who were wounded in their hearts and in their spirits, as well as in their bodies.

Now you might say, "Well, the guy should not have gone down the road to Jericho alone." You might say, "So what, he should have known that was a bad road. He should have known that when you leave Jerusalem and go down to Jericho, you drop right down to the bottom of the Dead Sea. There is a precipice on each side, and a thief can hide anywhere. He just should not have done that." I must admit that sounds very reasonable, but I must also tell you that there are times in life when things happen and no one could have avoided them.

I read a story in the newspaper about a man who was wanting to be very careful on the Fourth of July, so he stayed home. He decided that he would not get out on the highways because it was so dangerous, so he stayed in his back yard. The paper reported this: he was in the back yard when a small aircraft flew over. Somehow the door fell open and a tin can of spinach fell out and hit the guy on the head. I read about another man who fell in the bathtub and broke his arm. Now, can you say that the fellow should not have been in the back yard? Is it fair to say the fellow should not take a bath? No, I believe we would all agree that some things occur in life over which we have no control.

It happens. I do not understand all that happens to us. If I did, I would be God. Many times there is no human explanation.

I certainly do not believe, as some people, that God is being mean and nasty because He is a vengeful God. I simply think that many times the things which happen are just the result of living in this world. But when you are wounded, there is something you can do. If you are wounded, as you read this, I want to share with you three good statements to encourage you. Should you ever meet another who has been wounded, I ask you to give them these thoughts. I want you to help them to understand that the power of faith within them can help them to conquer their wounded spirit. Any doctor will tell you that half the battle of a patient getting well is that patient wanting to get well. Any preacher will tell you that half the battle of a person becoming a disciple of Jesus is that person wanting to be a disciple of Jesus.

I. YOU ARE NOT DEAD.

First of all, remember, to be wounded means YOU ARE NOT DEAD. It means you have not been killed. You are still alive. You still have something with which to fight. Through God's power you can still conquer, even though you have been hurt. People go through a time of divorce and it is a tragedy; it's like a death. Their soul is filled with anguish, and they are wounded deep inside, but they are not dead. You can fight back if you want to badly enough.

One of the great golf legends of the past was a man by the name of Ben Hogan. Even though I was very small, I remember hearing that Ben Hogan was in a terrible accident near Fort Worth, Texas. He was told by doctors, "You will never hit another golf ball in your life." Ben Hogan said, "I am not dead." Using a walker, he practiced swinging that club until he came back to win the U. S. Open and the British Open. Why? Because even though he was wounded, he was not dead.

In 1988, I took a sabbatical for ninety days. After pastoring large churches for almost thirty years, I was very tired. In 1987, in establishing Hillcrest Church, there was a time of "troubled waters." I took the blame personally.

The result was intense emotional and spiritual devastation. I was foolish in taking all the blame. There are always two sides to every broken relationship and truth lies somewhere in the middle. My critics and myself were both right on some issues and additionally, we were both right on other issues. Truth is never easy to find.

Maybe that is why Jesus was so specific - "You shall know the truth and the truth shall set you free." I have learned that on any issue, if you can ever discover the truth - you will be set free. It is the process of discovery that is so intense, often leaving us wounded emotionally.

If you have been wounded in your spirit, and if satan has tried to come against you to try to destroy you and to attack you mentally, then read the next sentence carefully. There is power in Jesus Christ, you do not have to give up, because Jesus is still able to heal your mind and your broken heart right now. Today!

In 1939 there was a submarine launched called the Squalus. On its first mission, its maiden voyage, it went 240 feet to the bottom of the ocean and smashed. Twenty-six men were killed; thirty-six survived. It is an interesting story because even though something went wrong with that submarine, it sank to the ocean floor, however, it was not totally destroyed. The government had a multi-million dollar investment, and somehow they were able to bring it up, salvage it, refurbish it, and commission it to serve again. In World War II it was renamed the Sailfish and put out to sea. Some of you who were in World War II might remember that it was the Sailfish submarine that battled through torrential typhoon waves and rains and brought down a twenty-two thousand ton enemy aircraft carrier. The same ship that had gone down in horrible defeat, rose again.

Why? Because my friend, to be injured is one thing, but it does not mean you must be stockpiled as worthless. As long as you have life within you, as long as somehow there is a fiber beating within the depth of your spirit, do not let satan tell you that you are defeated. You are not! You may be wounded; you may be side-tracked; you may be taken out of action for a while; but you do not have to stay there. The man on the Jericho road who was wounded had to rest for a while. He did not have to stay there forever.

II. HELP WILL COME.

Secondly, to be wounded means HELP WILL COME YOUR WAY. If you are wounded, you are not dead. That is number one. Number two, help will come your way. One Sunday a dear saint walked down the aisle of our church and said, "I am at the very end of my rope. I do not know what to do. I am in mental anguish and full of anxiety on the inside." As I prayed and counseled, the healing power of God flowed through that individual and help came to that person. The man who was by the wayside was wounded, but he was not completely left hopeless because there was help on the way. The Samaritan, a wretched social outcast, by society's standards of that day, stopped by the way and helped the man.

There is a painting by a man named Borthwick which shows a giant cathedral, and in the foreground there is a shabby lady who is making her way into that gigantic cathedral. Somehow the painter, Borthwick, is able to capture the essence of the presence of God as he shows His power coming down through the windows of the great cathedral and touching that shabby little piece of humanity. That troubled soul, that tattered and torn little lady is engulfed by the presence of God, and you sense in the painting that the power of God is raising that person up. Friend, you may be wounded, but you are not dead. Always remember that help is on the way!

We all face tough times when our mind is racked by pain and sorrow. Empty thoughts ricochet off the walls of our minds. "I am going crazy - I am losing my mind," we contemplate.

The ancient theologians had a term for this experience. They called it "the dark night of the soul." It seems that the meaning has something to do with a feeling of hopelessness and helplessness. I experienced "the dark night of the soul" in 1988 while on sabbatical.

I would wander around the house sensing an absence of God's presence. I tried to read God's Word. I tried to pray. Nothing worked. By determined faith, without any feelings, I survived one day at a time.

Years have passed. The wounds have been healed. The memories are intact, but the pain is gone.

Often, the very moment people say, "I give up" is the moment that Jesus walks into their lives. I feel God's presence upon every word that I am sharing with you because I know that I am writing as a dying man to dying men. I know that some of you have been wounded, hurt, and tormented. I know that you have wondered, "Why has this happened to me? God, what did I do to deserve this?" But, remember this. Jesus is with you as you are reading this right now. If you have been wounded, Jesus, through the power of the Holy Spirit, is reaching out to you, and He is healing you right now. Why? Because He knows that you are wounded and He wants to help you. Jesus never lets us fall all the way down. He somehow reaches out and pulls us up. I love the little verse by Elizabeth Chaney. She writes:

Said the robin to the sparrows, I would really like to know Why these anxious human beings rush about and worry so.

Said the Sparrow to the robin, Friend, I think that it must be, that they have no Heavenly Father such as cares for you and me.

You do have a Heavenly Father who cares for you. Number one, you may be wounded, but you are not dead. Number two, help is on the way. Now, I want to share with you thought number three.

III. DO NOT EVER BE BITTER.

My third thought for healing of a wounded spirit is DO NOT EVER BE BITTER. Bitterness is like a gigantic cancer. It eats away at the very internal structure of your soul. There is a verse by the writer of Hebrews that talks about this problem.

> *Look after each other so that no one of you will fail to find God's best blessings. Watch out that no bitterness takes root among you, for as it springs up it causes deep trouble, hurting many in their spiritual lives.*
>
> Hebrews 12:15 (Living Bible)

Here we are told that if there are any small roots of bitterness that begin to creep into our souls, we are headed for trouble. The moment you say, "God, I hate you. God, I did not deserve this," is the moment that bitterness creeps in.

There is a very interesting passage in Deuteronomy.

The passage indicates that bitterness of the inner man is related to anger with God. I personally believe that anger toward God is always present when bitterness is present. Bitterness is not a casual grudge. It is a lingering thought that says, "God has not been fair with me."

My father, a minister for over fifty years, tells about asking a West Texas farmer to give a testimonial of God's blessings.

The old man stood and blurted out, "God ain't been fair with me." He sat down. My dad was at a loss to know what to do. Then dad regained composure and explained that all of us feel that way at times. It is not the passing thought that creates the problem. It is the lingering thought of unfairness that produces anger, that produces bitterness.

There is a counseling technique called "reality therapy." The idea is that you must face your problems with realism. This approach to handling problems makes a lot of sense. It is time to face life realistically and when you have problems, say, "Jesus, I know that you are with me and by your stripes I am healed. I shall overcome this obstacle; I shall not be defeated." The power of God will touch you at that moment. Refuse to let bitterness creep in. Do not even let the root of bitterness get started.

Three names that have bill boarded Hollywood for decades are Metro-Goldwyn-Mayer. There is an interesting story about Louis Mayer, one of the three names. As a boy he was always filled with inferiority, and he was always fighting, always getting into trouble. One day he got the rough end of the deal and was beaten up pretty badly, and that night at home his mother heard him say, "Damn you, Bobby, I will get you tomorrow." Well, tomorrow happened to be a day that the family was going on a picnic.

They were out in the beauty of God's great terrestrial creation to enjoy the countryside, and the mother had a thought. She took her son to some nearby mountains. She said, "Son, last night I heard you say about your friend who beat you up, 'Damn you, Bobby.' Now, I want you to say that as loudly as you can to this mountain. I want you to scream it at the top of your lungs." The boy did not know why the mother was asking him to do that, but he cooperated. He screamed as loudly as he could, and in a few moments, the echo came ringing back, "Damn you."

Then the mother said, "Now, Son, I want you to say just as loudly, Bless you.'" In a few moments the echo came back, "Bless you!" That mother was somehow able to change her son's entire direction because she gave him a graphic illustration that you really get back quite often in life what you give out. The more bitter you are, the more bitterness you are going to receive. The more you sit around crying over your past experiences and weeping over all the bad deals you think God has given you, the more you are going to be filled with hatred, resentment, and bitterness. But the moment you break loose and let the presence of the Holy Spirit flow into you, you will be healed by the power of God.

IV. WHAT DO I DO??

Someone may be saying, I would love to be free as you say I can, but WHAT DO I DO? There is a story in the book of Numbers, chapter 13, which I would like you to read. In this story we find twelve men who went over into the promised land, Israel, to spy out the land. The grapes were luscious and beautiful. They had to carry them back on long poles with two men carrying the poles. When they came back, Moses said, "What is the report?"

"Oh, you have never seen such grapes. There are grapes so big that we had to get two men to put a bunch on a stick to carry it back. You have never in all your travels seen anything like this. I tell you, Moses, we have never seen grapes like those grapes in Canaan." "Oh, that's wonderful. We will have something to eat when we conquer the land," Moses said. "Well, yes," they said, "but, but, but, Moses, there is a little, slight problem. They do not have ordinary farmers who tend those grape vineyards. Giants grow the grapes. Now the grapes are luscious, but you should see the giants that take care of the vineyard. That is our problem, right there."

Caleb, who was listening to this report, was an ordinary "John Doe." He stood up and said, "That is all true. Those grapes really were delicious. And we had grape juice that was beyond description. And, yes, there are giants like you have never seen before in your life. There are real giants! But the Lord wants us to possess the land."

God is saying to someone right now who has a wounded spirit, "Get your eyes off the giants and start looking at the grapes." If you take that analogy down the road a little way you will conclude that when you have grapes, you can make wine. If you can be filled with a new wine of the Holy Spirit, you can stand up and look at those grapes instead of looking at the giants. So I want to ask you. Is it grapes or giants? Which will it be in your life? Perhaps you are thinking, "Well, that's right. Caleb is speaking the truth, but remember the giants are so big that we look like grasshoppers."

A lot of folk today have a grasshopper complex. They feel so inferior, they are constantly compelled to jump from one objective to another in an attempt to diminish their feelings of inferiority. I want you to know that Jesus desires to heal you of inferiority because many times that is a result of a wounded spirit. God wants to set you free from bitterness and inferiority and give you the courage to hold your chin up high when you have been hurt and say, "Praise God! I do not understand what has happened to me. I do not know why this has to come my way, but I will not be defeated. I am wounded. I am not dead. I know that help is on the way. I refuse to be bitter. I am going to keep on being filled with a new wine of the Kingdom of God."

Would you like to know something interesting about that little story? There were two who had a positive report and ten who had a negative report. That is two to ten, or to break it down mathematically, that is a one to five ratio and that has not changed in six thousand years. There is still a one to five ratio because you have five senses:

your hearing, sight, smelling, taste, and feeling. Those five senses still try to operate against the one great truth which is the Word of God. As long as you proceed on the same ratio of one to five, you are going to be defeated just like Israel was. As long as you keep going around letting your circumstances buffet you, and allowing your five senses to tell you what to do, you are going to be defeated. But the moment you stand up and say, "Oh, thank God. World, I want you to know though everything is against me, though it looks bad, though I hear bad things, though I am in bad circumstances, I am going to stand on the truth of God's Word which says that in Jesus Christ, I am more than a conqueror and I shall not be defeated!" He is the One Who overcomes all five.

God wants to heal you who have a wounded spirit right now. Get your eyes off giants, start looking for grapes to make wine. Wine is a beautiful symbol of the Spirit, and God wants you to become so filled with the Holy Spirit that the old wounded spirit will have to flee. It will have to leave. If you will allow Him, the Spirit of God is going to do a healing work. There can be an instantaneous healing as you prayerfully read this right now, and people who have wounded spirits can be made whole by the power of God. If you will step out and believe in the power of God, the miraculous power of the Spirit to do the healing work, Jesus will heal you right now. Believe it! Believe it!

CHAPTER 4

BROKEN DREAMS

For which cause also I have been much hindered from coming to you. But now having no more place in these parts, and having a great desire these many years to come unto you: Whensoever I take my journey into Spain, I will come to you: for I trust to see you in my journey, and to be brought on my way thitherward by you, if first I be somewhat filled with your company.

But now I go into Jerusalem to minister unto the saints. For it hath pleased them of Macedonia and Achaia to make a certain contribution for the poor saints which are at Jerusalem. It hath pleased them verily; and their debtors they are. For if the Gentiles have been made partakers of their spiritual things, their duty is also to minister unto them in carnal things.

> *When therefore, I have performed this, and have sealed to them this fruit, I will come by you into Spain.*
>
> Romans 15

There is probably not a person reading this who at some time has not felt the pain of a broken dream. A shattered hope, an ambition you had worked for which you somehow knew was going to take place, but then it did not happen. This is the story we have in Romans 15. For deep within the inner being of the apostle Paul was a deep desire to go to Spain. He dreamed of reaching the farthest western point of the Roman Empire. As I read the writings of the Apostle Paul, I see him as a very ambitious man, though humble. A man with a tremendous amount of inner energy and drive who wanted to conquer every known area for Jesus Christ. I liken the apostle Paul to Alexander the Great, for Alexander dreamed of the Grecian Empire being stretched all the way from Greece to Egypt. So it must have been in the heart of the apostle Paul to see that the Gospel could go forward to even the farthest point, the land of Spain.

No doubt he was thinking about the power of Spain at this time. From Spain had come some great men. Seneca, the Roman Senator, was a Spaniard. Also, Lucian, the great poet and philosopher, had been born and reared in Spain. And Paul dreamed of going to Spain and preaching the Gospel. But his dream ended in a prison cell in Rome. After having taken the collection from the churches to the Jerusalem saints (who were in trouble because of severe famine), Paul was taken prisoner. Instead of being able to make his way to Spain by going through Rome, as he had written to the Romans, his journey ended up in Rome, but in the bottom of the Roman prison. Broken dreams, the apostle Paul knew about them.

I feel sure almost every person reading this has experienced the disappointment of a broken dream somewhere along the way, or if you have not, no doubt you will. There are two approaches you can take to broken dreams. There are two ways in which you can react. You can either become bitter or you can become better. It is entirely up to you. You have the decision, you have the choice. When a dream is shattered on the sidewalk of life, you have to decide. Am I going to become bitter and let this thing gnaw away at me and destroy me or am I going to stand up and become better? It is up to you.

I. JUDAS, A BITTER MAN

The first man I would like to study is in Matthew, chapter 27. It is a very interesting and intriguing story of a man who had a dream.

> *Then Judas, which had betrayed him, when he saw that he was condemned, repented himself, and brought again the thirty pieces of silver to the chief priests and elders, Saying, I have sinned in that I have betrayed innocent blood. And they said, What is that to us? See thou to that. And he cast down the pieces of silver in the temple, and departed, and went and hanged himself.*
>
> Matthew 27

I am fully convinced in studying the life of Judas Iscariot, that he lived with a broken dream. I believe Judas dreamed of a Messianic Kingdom. That is not hard to understand because all the Jews dreamed of a Messianic Kingdom. They dreamed of the day when Messiah would come and He would be so powerful and great that He would overthrow the Roman armies which were oppressing the Jewish people. The Jewish people dreamed of that Messianic hope, that day of the Kingdom, that glorious hour. Oh, yes, friend, according to Revelation chapter 20, that Messianic hope shall still take place and there shall still be a Messianic Kingdom of Jesus reigning upon the earth. But in Judas' day the timing was wrong. Yet, he believed, hoped, and dreamed for it, and when he saw his dream being slowly but surely shattered, he threw himself in with the opposing forces for a few pieces of silver. He sold out his soul.

But the Bible says in Matthew 3:27 that he repented. In the Greek, it is a word which means, Judas was extremely remorseful for his guilt. However, there is no indication anywhere in the Scripture that he was ever remorseful to God. He was only remorseful within himself. He was only hating himself because of his guilt for what he had done. He never once repented to the Father. A broken dream, a shattered hope, and a bitter spirit resulted in taking his own life outside the Jerusalem walls.

There is a very powerful passage in Hebrews which gives us these words of wisdom.

Follow peace with all men, and holiness, without which no man shall see the Lord: Looking diligently lest any man fail of the grace of God; lest any root of bitterness springing up trouble you, and thereby many be defiled.

Hebrews 12:14,15

The writer of Hebrews says, "Oh, listen, follow peace with all men, seek the Lord, fail not, and remember, never let a root of bitterness spring up inside of you." That root of bitterness which begins very small, begins to grow like a cancerous sore. Before long you find yourself malignant, spiritually speaking, because inside of you, you have allowed bitterness to creep in. A dream you had hoped for, some friend who broke your confidence, some marriage difficulty, some financial reverse that turned your life upside down, something that you had longed for and hoped for, suddenly smashed on the pavement of life.

A LITTLE BITTERNESS CREEPS IN - just a little bit at first. But you nourish that bitterness through self-pity. You still long to have your dreams fulfilled even though they have been shattered. Then you begin to say, "God, I do not deserve this," and bitterness begins to grow.

Two things happen when you develop a root of bitterness. Hebrews 12, verse 15 says, first of all you personally will be troubled as a result of the bitterness springing up inside of you and secondly those around you shall be defiled. This means they shall be made burdensome because of your root of bitterness.

It happened to Vincent Foster, President Clinton's Deputy Counsel. He left a suicide note that read - "Washington D.C. is a place where lives are ruined. People (newspapers) lie against you, with no conscience." Mr. Foster, reportedly a faithful public servant, allowed the lies of others to destroy his life.

I know. It can happen. A media medium can tell a half-truth and the public believes a lie.

It happened to me in 1978 when I ran for the United States Congress. A printed lie in a small town paper was systematically distributed across the entire district one week before the election. I was in striking distance in the polls to win. I lost.

Thank God. I instantly decided to be a better man, not a bitter man. I could have been bitter.

How many men have destroyed their own families because they have allowed a root of bitterness to creep in about something in their employment, and they let that grow and grow until it became a spiritual malignancy defiling their own family? How many women have let shattered dreams of the kind of a home they had longed for cause bitterness to spring up and begin to grow inside of them? Not only will you be defiled (it would be one thing if just you were defiled), but the bitterness never stops with one. It always defiles someone else. Shattered dreams. Disappointed hopes. If you want, you can become bitter like Judas Iscariot - OR - you can decide to become better.

II. PAUL, A BETTER MAN

The story is told in II Corinthians chapter 11 of a man who chose to be better rather than bitter.

> *Of the Jews five times received I forty stripes save one. Thrice was I beaten with rods, once was I stoned, thrice I suffered shipwreck, a night and a day I have been in the deep. In journeyings often, in perils of waters, in perils of robbers, in perils by mine own countrymen, in perils by the heathen, in perils in the city, in perils in the wilderness, in perils in the sea, in perils among false brethren; In weariness and painfulness, in watchings often, in hunger, thirst, in fastings often, in cold and nakedness...If I must needs glory, I will glory of the things which concern mine infirmities. The God and Father of our Lord Jesus*

Christ, which is blessed forevermore, knoweth that I lie not.
II Corinthians 11:24-27, 30-31

The apostle Paul shipwrecked, beaten, hungry, starving, maliciously treated says, "I lie not. I am telling you the truth." Paul did not become bitter. He refused; instead he became BETTER. There are several things in life you can do to keep from becoming bitter. I want to suggest some of them for you right now. These are simple steps to help you.

1. You must decide.

You must decide whether you are going to be bitter or better. You say, "Pastor Sheats, it is not that simple. You do not understand. I am in a situation over which I have no control." That may be true. A young man wrote me from jail not too long ago, saying, "I am in the bonds of prison, but I am not spiritually in bondage because I see the light of Jesus." You see, even though he could do nothing to change that situation, he had chosen not to become bitter. You can decide whether you are going to be bitter or whether you are going to be better when your dreams are disappointed. It is your decision.

The power of decision should never be underestimated. "As a man thinks in his heart, so is he." You must decide.

I was able to slowly come to a decision after several stinging defeats in my life.

I remember one in particular. I was leading Trinity Church in Lubbock, Texas in its first major building campaign. The big beams were delayed in shipping and the construction manager said he could not wait.

Hastily I told him to build my family a house on a lot we owned. Without proper prayer, without proper evaluation, we proceeded.

Soon the beams came in and the building at the church building took precedence in my mind, over the building of our home. It was a cost-ly mistake. However, I was only twenty-eight years old. I learned.

We lost the house and had to sell it below market price to get a quick transaction. The money lost had to be repaid at the bank for several years.

I moved my family from our dream home of 3,400 square feet to a little cottage of 1,400 square feet.

Fortunately, my wife and I decided not to be defeated in our emotions and mind. When dreams are shattered, you must decide to conquer rather than be conquered.

A woman found herself in the Mojave Desert with her husband, a sergeant in the United States Army. He was there on special army maneuvers. She hated the place. Sand and filth everywhere, and as she put it, the only other people were "a bunch of old Indians." She wrote her father back in the East, where she had been sumptuously raised in an atmosphere of elegance. She was complaining bitterly of her lot in life and where she was. Her father, with real wisdom, wrote back to his daughter and said, "Two men looked out from prison bars. One saw the mud; the other saw the stars." You can decide whether you are going to be bitter or better. That is the first step: Decide. Decide you are not going to be defeated.

2. Saturate your mind with thoughts of God.

Day and night, pour the truth of God's Word into your mind. Read it, meditate upon it, turn it over in your mind and press it down. Realize there is life in this Word and somehow as you begin to saturate your soul with this Truth, the bitterness begins to flow out.

Those are pretty simple steps, but how many people totally ignore them? When something happens, they refuse to decide. But you must decide - bitter or better. You decide you are not going to be defeated; you decide that as a Christian you are not going to give up. Oh, there may be times when you will be flat on your face. There may be times when you will be crawling in the mud of life, but do not ever stop crawling. As long as you are moving, there is hope, and if you fall flat on your face, get one elbow back up and keep on going. There is no reason in this life to let any dream that has been shattered among us, defeat us, for in Christ Jesus there is hope beyond this life. We cannot give up and quit the battle. If we saturate our minds with the Word, we have the Sword that will win the battle.

I have watched my wife, Janet, battle Multiple Sclerosis for fifteen years. Her neurologist told me when he first diagnosed her that she was so bad that she would live no more than five years.

In 1983, she experienced a remarkable healing. It came through our children reading God's Word to her. Her eyesight was greatly deteriorated by the disease, so Shanda and Mo read to her in two shifts each evening.

The saturation of the mind and spirit produced a slow healing in Janet's body. Even though the healing has not yet been totally complete, she is still alive. All praise to God.

3. Ask God's forgiveness.

There is one more step I want to suggest in overcoming bitterness. First, you must decide. Secondly, saturate yourself with the Word of God. And thirdly, ask God's forgiveness for bitterness, because bitterness is a sin. You say, "I don't like that." I love it, because there is life in Christ when you confess your sins and bitterness is a sin.

Let me share with you a beautiful passage from the Living Bible concerning God's forgiveness. Listen to this.

> *What happiness for those whose guilt has been forgiven! What joys when sins are covered over! What relief for those who have confessed their sins and God has cleared their record.*
> *There was a time when I wouldn't admit what a sinner I was. But my dishonesty made me miserable and filled my days with*

frustration. All day and all night your hand was heavy on me. My strength evaporated like water on a sunny day until I finally admitted all my sins to you and stopped trying to hide them. I said to myself, "I will confess them to the Lord." And you forgave me! All my guilt is gone.

Psalm 32:1-4

As long as you refuse to admit you have bitterness, you are going to continue in bitterness. In other words as long as you carry bitterness around, you are carrying sin around. As long as you are carrying sin around, your strength is going to evaporate like the showers on the pavement on a sunny day. Some of you think you are tired because you have vitamin problems. You may be tired because you have spiritual problems. Say to yourself, "I will confess them to the Lord, these sins of mine. I am going to confess thanks to God, you forgive me, and now all my guilt is gone."

III. CAUSES OF BITTERNESS

Many times, we become bitter because we have unrealistic dreams in life. If your goals, your priorities, or your dreams are unrealistic, many times, that will automatically result in a broken dream, which will automatically result in bitterness. So now, I feel compelled to try to help you to know how to establish proper priorities or proper dreams. Let me give you some suggestions for establishing proper priorities or proper dreams.

1. You must determine your priorities.

You will never be happy, you will never find any stability in a marriage, in a business, or in a church until you decide what is important. You must decide, "What is my first priority?"

2. You must be willing to adjust your priorities as the Holy Spirit

leads you.

You begin with one priority which you feel is important, but you must be willing to adjust your priority as the Holy Spirit leads you.

I am concerned when writing about priorities that a sense of legalism may be the result. For this reason, I stress the adjusting of your priorities by the leadership of the Holy Spirit.

Organized flexibility may be the best way to describe the process. Prior planning prevents poor performance. However, it is possible to be so well organized as to miss the leadership of the Holy Spirit. Plan, but be flexible.

3. Live by Philippians 4:11-13.

> *Not that I speak in respect of want: for I have learned in whatsoever state I am, therewith to be content. I know both how to be abased, and I know how to abound: everywhere and in all things I am instructed both to be full and to be hungry, both to abound and to suffer need.*
>
> Philippians 4:11,12

I have had great blessings, Paul says. I have had luxury. I have had abundance; and I have also had nothing, but I have learned how to live.

> *I can (CAN - capitalize it six feet tall) I CAN do all things through Christ which strengtheneth me.*
>
> Philippians 4:13

If you are one who has undefined, confusing priorities, I would beg of you to sit down and write out what God is saying should be your priorities. Know Jesus. Know Him in the fullness of His power. The Bible says in Colossians 1:3, "In Jesus Christ are hid all the treasures of wisdom and knowledge." You want wisdom; you want knowledge, then let Jesus be your first priority and He will give you wisdom and knowledge. When that happens all the rest of your priorities will fall in line.

Decide what your priorities are; decide to be willing to adjust as the Holy Spirit leads you, and live by Philippians 4:11-13. Then when the shattered and broken dreams of life come, we can decide - we will not become bitter - we will become better.

CHAPTER 5

THE HIDDEN CHILD WITHIN YOU

But when that which is perfect is come, then that which is in part shall be done away. When I was a child, I spake as a child, I understtod as a child,I thought as a child: but when I became a man, I put away childish things.

I Corinthians 13:10-11

And he gave some, apostles; and some, prophets; and some, evangelists; and some pastors and teachers; for the perfecting of the saints, for the work of the ministry, for the edifying of the body of Christ: till we all come in the unity of the faith, and of the knowledge of the Son of God, unto a perfect man, unto the measure of the stature of the fullness of Christ: that we henceforth be no more children, tossed to and fro, and carried about with every wind of doctrine, by the sleight of men, and cunning craftiness, whereby they lie in wait to deceive; but speaking the truth in love, may grow up into him in all things, which is the head, even Christ.

Ephesians 4:11-15

The very first sermon that Jesus ever preached in his home church was one that went like this:

The Spirit of the Lord is upon me. I have come to preach the

gospel and set at liberty those who are in captivity.
                                  Luke 4:18-19 (Paraphrase)

More and more God is showing us that when we set people free from their respective captivity, we are indeed preaching the gospel. Whether it be captivity to sin, captivity to something that happened years ago, or captivity to the entirety of one's past, men can be set free by the power of the living God. The good news is freedom in Christ Jesus.

There are many good, solid Christians who are defeated in their walk every day. They believe that God is real, but somehow they have not been able to appropriate the power of God in their individual lives. The apostle Paul tells us that we are spirit, soul, and body. We are not segmented - we do not come to church on Sunday and deal only with the spirit; similarly, we do not dedicate Monday to dealing with our bodies, nor do we set aside Wednesday for the feeding and repair of the soul or mind. We are all three parts: spirit, soul, and body. We must seek wholeness. We must allow the seed within us to have a growing-up experience. The apostle Paul, in writing to the church in Ephesus, says:

> *We are no longer to be children, tossed by the waves and whirled about by every fresh gust of teaching, dupes of crafty rogues and their deceitful schemes.*
>   Ephesians 4:14, The New English Bible

We are to "no longer be children." Are you aware of the one ingredient it takes to grow up and be strong? The ingredient is love. If we are ever to be mature, we must learn to love. This is what the Bible says:

> *When I was a child, I spake as a child, I understood as a child, I thought as a child: but when I became a man I put away childish things.*
>   I Corinthians 13:11

One of the great misconceptions we entertain is that people automatically grow in maturity because they grow physically. Nothing could be farther from the truth. There are many people who, as far as chronological progress is concerned, are mature. But when emotions and spiritual matters are taken into account, they may still be infants, even though they have been in church for years.

A long time ago, God put a story in the New Testament about some men working in the fields. The first worked all day; the second worked half a day; the third worked one hour. Each man received the same wage. I used to wonder how such an unjust story ever worked its way into the Bible until one day I began to understand the spiritual truths, one of which is that God uses people who have only been in the walk a half a day, a quarter of a day, or even an hour. In many cases, He uses them in a much more mature manner than some Christians who have been in the walk all their lives. Spiritual maturity is not based on time - it comes from godly character.

Trees grow and sprout their leaves in spring, lose their leaves in fall, and automatically regain them the next spring. Many of us believe that when people grow up they are like the leaves; if they happen to lose out along the way, they will grow back. Unfortunately, it is not that simple.

Notice what the Apostle Paul says: "When I became a man, I put away childish things." The phrase "put away" is one word in Greek: "Katargeo." A very strong word, it means "to render inoperative or to take the meaning out of something." Mainly it means "to set free or to rip out by the roots." Paul uses the same word in Romans.

> *Knowing this, that our old man is crucified with him, that the body of sin might be (Katargeo) destroyed, that henceforth we should not serve sin.*
>
> Romans 6:6

Someone is probably thinking, "That sounds great, Pastor, but how can I cut my childish nature out? How can I destroy the child within?" There are several things we need to remember. They may seem somewhat unnecessary, but look at them closely. Most profound truth is simple.

I. THE CHILD MAY STILL DWELL WITHIN US.

First, every one of us has, at one time, been a child. We have all known the glory and frustration of that personal era known as childhood. THE CHILD WE ONCE WERE MAY STILL DWELL WITHIN US. The Scriptures say:

> *A little child shall lead them.*
>
> Isaiah 11:6

We tend to think of that child as a little boy or girl. Another interpretation would be the little boy or girl within us. Sometimes the child within is there to lead us, but all too often the child within is there to mislead us. You are a tapestry of the past, woven together by your childhood, adolescent, and adult years, and the hidden child within you may be the determining factor within your life.

Many children are obnoxious - bullies, if you will. Their favorite preoccupation is making other children miserable. As one person said to me not long ago, "When I was a kid, I constantly pushed people around. I was afraid. I did not know what to do with myself. I just elbowed my way through life." Other children are extremely shy and unobtrusive. At a gathering of peers, they go to a corner and sit there by themselves. Why? Because they feel intimidated by life; they feel no security.

> *And I, brethren, could not speak unto you as unto spiritual, but as unto carnal, even as unto babes in Christ. I have fed you with milk, and not with meat; for hitherto ye were not able to bear it, neither yet now are ye able. For ye are yet carnal: for whereas there is among you envying, and strife, and divisions, are ye not carnal, and walk as men?*
>
> I Corinthians 3:1-3

Thus, the apostle Paul continues in a further discourse on the carnal or childish nature in many Christians. Some of us, he is saying, have failed to grow up - we are still infants. Each of us, at one time or another, has applied this thinking to the spiritual man. We have said, "In the church there are those who are childish and there are those who are spiritual." Many times envy, strife, and division run rampant because that little child is still within us, and he has the dangerous potential of becoming a bully or a spineless milquetoast even though his dwelling may be a grown adult.

A lady came to see me one time. She shared her driven spirit to shop constantly. "My house is full already, yet I shop." We talked about her childhood and discovered she was raised in poverty as a child. She determined as a child that someday she would have lots of "things."

As an adult, however, she realized the utter futility of amassing material goods. Unfortunately she married a man from the same background of poverty. He too was driven. He even built extra garages as an adult to house his expensive cars. Both were quite unfulfilled.

In prayer one day, the lady asked if God could heal the child within her. In conversational prayer, the gracious healing power of God made her whole.

Her absence of pointless shopping astounded her husband. He was pleased, yet unwilling to be healed himself. He wanted his toys more than he wanted wholeness.

II. GOD WANTS TO HEAL YOU OF THE CHILD WITHIN.

Now, what does God want to do about all this? GOD WANTS TO HEAL YOU OF THE CHILD WITHIN. There is a child somewhere in your past; that child continues to live somewhere in your life. We need to expose him and find out where and why he is defeating us. By the power of the Holy Spirit, we need to "katargeo" that child. When we have destroyed him, we can grow into mature love. We can become adults not only physically but spiritually. It is imperative that we discover him and, by the might of God's Holy Spirit, cut him out. We need to render him so absolutely ineffective that we can move in the world as spiritual and authoritative adults in Christ Jesus.

While on the campus of Southern Baptist Seminary in Louisville, Kentucky, a few years ago, I was walking with a young pastor from Georgia. He started weeping. I said, "What is the matter? Did I say something wrong?"

"No, not at all," he said. "It's just that, in the last session one of the speakers said, If there is anyone you hate, get rid of that hatred or it will keep coming out and you will find yourself hating people you do not really want to hate. You will find it coming out and you will react, and it will not be because they are the person they are - it will be because something inside is eating away at your inner being!"

He wept quietly for a moment, then looked at me and said, "For years I've hated my father. I've hated him. And now he's gone. I can't go and say now, 'I have hated you, father. Please forgive me.'"

"What are you going to do?"

He wiped his face with a handkerchief, "I'm in a very successful church. Things are generally pretty good, but sometimes when a father figure - one of my good deacons - tries to counsel me, I react; and I've even found hatred welling up inside of me. And now I understand. It's not them at all; it's my father. I'm going to have a funeral service right here, Morris."

"Will you help me bury my dad?"

We stopped in the middle of the campus. We took one another's hands, and we prayed a burial prayer over that father who had been dead for so long. Afterward, hatred dwelt in that young man's life no longer. He wrote me much later to describe his freedom from hatred. This is proof of the fact that the Lord, by His Holy Spirit, wants to heal our past.

Let me make a caution at this point. Someone may be thinking, "I guess Pastor Sheats wants me to go back and dig through all my childhood experiences - when my brother broke my doll, when my sister put bubble gum in my hair, and all that." On the contrary - the only thing this produces is the syndrome known as "paralysis of analysis." One can analyze up to a point, and then he becomes paralyzed. People have spent countless thousands of dollars trying to figure out who they were when they were three years old, and they have never been healed. Occasionally, we think, "I wouldn't be this way if that Marlon Brando type hadn't jilted me in '54." This kind of thinking is pure rationalization, and it is time we buried it in the seas of God's forgetfulness. We must reclaim our spines and say, "I do not care where I was reared; I do not care what happened to me - I refuse to be directed by that childish nature any longer." The power of God can then mold you into the kind of man or woman you need to be.

I shall never forget a visit to my grandmother's when I was a teenager. I had always thought I had a very cute dimple on one side of my face. I would look in the mirror and smile. I liked that dimple. I was proud of it. And then one day, in conversation, my grandmother casually mentioned that she had dropped me on the stove when I was an infant. I was not born with that dimple - I received it from the stove. I could have gone into a great trauma at this point and shrieked, "I have been deceived!" Many people do that, you know. Some of us uncover something that happened to us a long time ago and become exceedingly upset. That is ridiculous. It is time we stopped blaming the way we are on things that happened to us years ago. It is no longer the age when we can say, "It was my environment - if it had been better, I would be better." You can only be different when you decide to let the Holy Spirit make you different. He is the Power by which we can be changed - and changed permanently.

Praise God for Christian counselors, men and women, who love God deeply and are Spirit-filled. But all the counseling and analysis in the world will never change you and free you from what you used to be like a touch from the Holy Spirit.

III. AREAS WHERE THE CHILD CAN BE SEEN

My experience, both personally and in years of counseling, has shown me that the AREAS WHERE THE CHILD CAN BE SEEN most readily will be the situations we share with those whom we love the most. The child seems to realize that he cannot emerge in public; he knows that a thirty-five year old man does not throw himself on the floor and enter into a bellowing tantrum. When, however, we move out of the range of the public eye, that hard shell does not have to be there any more. Home - field of marital and parental relations - is where we will generally find the child, because home is where we relax and see that we do not have to be the way we have been all day long. The wife will accept you if you are a little nasty; the kids will like you even if you get a little grouchy. It is usually in the relationship between a man and wife that the child comes out. Remember, in marriage, four people are united, two adults and two kids. When we marry, we have not grown into complete adulthood, although we may be chronologically of age. The child within us may still be very active.

1. Marriage

Watch very carefully the situation in which you react in a negative way, for here you will find that the child will usually emerge in one of three areas in your marriage: money, sex, or disciplining of the children.

A man once said to me, "I don't know what to do. I love my wife very deeply. All day long I think about her when I'm working. I want to make her happy. But when I get home, something happens; I don't act the way I planned to act all day long. Something goes wrong and I'm just like a little kid again. Instead of acting, I find myself reacting." All too often we find ourselves reacting to situations because the child is threatened. We tend to fight back and say sardonic things because the child is rearing its head again.

I remember a day (there have been many) when I came in and let my guard down. One of the children did something I did not particularly like, and because he challenged my authority, I promptly endowed him with a liberal spanking. Because my wife and I maintained a policy never to disagree before the children, it was not until later that she said, "Why did you react like that?" "I don't know," I replied helplessly. "I simply don't know." I began to think about the whole thing, and my mind wandered back to my childhood and the times I had felt threatened by authority. No doubt my reaction was a result of the child's threatened nature - the child within me.

2. Speech

Consider your speech. Many adults actually speak like children. When a child is caught in a "crime," he will usually go into a profound oration involving all the reasons for his action. "Well, I'll tell you," my little boy once told me. "I did it because Susanne made me do it." I consulted Susanne. She said Mo made her do it. All I knew was that someone had spilled five gallons of paint on the driveway!

A petty occurrence, you might say. Perhaps. But petty occurrences often evolve into serious incidents. Someday a child grows up. Someday something goes wrong, and instead of saying, "Yes, I'm responsible," the individual says, "I wouldn't have done it if that guy over there hadn't got me involved." Parents must train the child to prevent future rebellion and actions that could lead to serious trouble for the child, as an adult.

Do you know what Jesus said about speech? "Let your yes be yes and your no be no." If we would pay attention to that, our lives would be much less complicated. If we could stop our vacillating between yes and no, confusion would dwindle to a minimum.

My children broke me of the vacillating habit. When they would ask me something, I'd say "maybe." Finally it got to the point they would say, "Don't say maybe, say yes or no." This is what we must do: make up our minds.

When we do a poor job on something, are we going to rationalize? Or are we going to say, "I am sorry. Thanks for calling it to my attention; it will not happen again."

3. Attitudes

"When I was a child...I understood as a child." I've learned from years of pastoring that there are too many people with childish attitudes. I sit down to counsel with them and very soon I realize it is not going to be an easy session, because their attitude is that of a child. In the Christian walk, we can strangle that attitude by facing reality. Life is not always peaches and cream; it is not always marvelous. But,with a good attitude, life can be taken by the throat. You can succeed!

When the Holy Spirit breathes on you, when He touches a part of your life, when He makes you realize that you have been acting a certain way because a part of you needs healing - then you can fall to your knees and praise God. You do not have to go through three years of psychoanalysis. Simply ask God to heal you. Ask Him to "katargeo" the child that generates all the misery within you - ask Him to cut it out. And when He has destroyed it, thank Him for enabling you to walk as a man. A mature adult.

One more caution: do not imagine things that are not there. You may have it better than you realize. Do not start creating problems. Do not put this down and say, "Pastor Sheats said I have to find something wrong with myself this week." I did not say that. But if you know that you do have a definite hindrance in your life, talk to God. He will hear you and He will help you. That is a promise.

> *And whatsoever ye shall ask in my name, that will I do, that the Father may be glorified in the Son. If ye shall ask any thing in*

my name, I will do it.

John 14:13, 14

Let the child die. Let God set up housekeeping in your heart.

CHAPTER 6

SPIRITUAL ANSWERS TO FINANCIAL PROBLEMS

I read with interest a report of seven top psychiatrists who concluded that: "Due to the recession, families are crumbling under the pressure of resentment and fear. Workers are developing bad attitudes toward their jobs. People are becoming financially reckless, flinging away their money. More and more Americans are being forced to seek psychiatric help; anger is mounting, and the mood of the people is potentially explosive."

Dr. Jack Churness, Assistant Professor of Psychiatry, New Jersey College of Medicine, Newark, states, "Every aspect of family life is being affected by financial problems."

First, families must give up luxuries and then they are forced to worry about how they will pay for necessities. The psychiatric director of the Institute of Group Dynamics of New York said, "Because people feel they cannot move from job to job as they used to, people are depressed and they are angry at work." He also said the diminishing dollar is making people reckless about their money. The prevalent attitude is, "What the heck, the buck is worthless anyhow." Not only are the financially irresponsible affected, but those people who have been thrifty all their lives, putting away every spare penny, are having the most reckless reactions of all. All their efforts seem to them to be doomed, and sacrifices they have made through the years have been for naught.

Dr. Samuel Silverman, a psychiatrist at Harvard Medical School, predicts the problems of supporting a family will be emotionally crippling and Dr. Barbara Bevin, a prominent Los Angeles psychiatrist, states that people will soon say to themselves, "I am going to feed my family, no matter how I have to do it." Crimes will be committed as a last resort, and a breakdown of law looms ahead. Are we already there?

America, that is a rather distressing report from seven major psychiatrists. The answer appears to be simple. In fact, I hear people everywhere proclaiming, "If we only had more money. That would be the answer." You know, years ago that is what Solomon believed. In the book of Ecclesiastes, which follows the book of Proverbs, you might want to notice something that Solomon said. This man who was immensely wealthy, this man who had seemingly all the world at his fingertips said this:

> *A feast is made for laughter, and wine maketh merry: but money answereth all things.*
>
> Ecclesiastes 10:19

Now, if we stopped there, it would seem that the great intellectual giant Solomon believed that the answer to all our needs is a simple thing called money. And we would agree that in view of the swings from recession to inflation, which we all confront today, that more money seems to be the solution. But, friends, Ecclesiastes goes on to record the later writings of this very wise man. Solomon declares:

> *Let us hear the conclusion of the whole matter; Fear God, and keep His commandments; for this is the whole duty of man. For God shall bring every work into judgment, with every secret thing, whether it be good or whether it be evil.*
>
> Ecclesiastes 12:13

Evidently, Solomon learned somewhere during the course of his life that money is not really the answer to everything. He concluded all his travel, all of his intellectual pursuits, the summation of his lifetime, with these words, "Let us hear the conclusion of the entire matter. Fear God and keep His commandments."

The age is now upon us when the answer to our problems is not having more money. The answer to our problem is to learn how to fear God and to keep His commandments. In studying Philippians, chapter 4, God has said to me in no uncertain terms, "Here are the principles wherein my people can stand in difficult days." Here are the principles you can hold onto when times are difficult; when each day seems to pull more and more at your pocketbook; when as you go to the grocery store, you can only buy less and less. What are you going to hang onto? Is the answer in walking out of your marriage? Is the answer walking off you job? Is the answer saying, "What's the use?" Frankly, all of these "answers" were spawned in the pit of hell itself, because satan is trying to capitalize upon this hour in which we are living. The time has come when we must say, "I will stand upon the Word of God; I will fear God; I will keep His commandments. No matter what may come, I am going to refuse to be defeated." When you take this kind of a position and you base your life on Philippians, chapter 4, you will be strong.

I. STAND FAST IN THE LORD.

The first principle is this: STAND FAST IN THE LORD. Verse 1 of Philippians, chapter 4 says for us to stand fast in the Lord. I have come to the place in life where I believe everything in this life is temporary except God. I said, "EVERYTHING." Churches can blow away, people can move, confidences can be broken, banks can go under, financial disaster can hit, the stock market can drop lower than it has in many years, but I tell you God is still alive and He is still on the throne. Therefore, I am going to stand fast in the Lord. I am going to base my life on Him.

A dear friend of mine recently experienced disaster in a project he had worked on for many months. He had given every waking hour both mentally and physically to the construction of a rehabilitation center. Just as completion was in sight and dedicatory plans were being made, fire struck in the wee hours of the morning, and all his labor quickly went up in smoke. However, you never see God go up in smoke. You see His hand upon this universe day in and day out, month in and month out, year in and year out. The hand of the Lord rests upon us, and in Him you can stand!

Folks come and they go. Ideas come and they go. People live and people die; we breathe and we pass off the stage of action; we make our entrance and we make our exit. But I want you to know the hand of God is everlasting; He is the beginning and the end, and I am going to stand on Him.

> *Trust in the Lord and lean not unto your own understanding.*
> *In all thy ways acknowledge Him and He shall direct thy paths.*
> Proverbs 3:5-6

II. HELP ONE ANOTHER

The second principle we can stand on in these recessionary days is the principle of HELPING ONE ANOTHER. In verses two and three of Philippians chapter 4, Paul says, "Help Euodias and Syntyche and Clement and those who helped me." I believe days have come when the saints of God are going to have to stand together. We are going to have to help each other, and we're going to have to share the things that God blesses us with. Our love for one another must be so strong that if we have a need, if we are in trouble, we will automatically turn to the body of believers for help rather than anyone else. That day is now here. We are learning to share our food; we are learning to share our houses; we are learning to share our cars; it is a principle ordained of God. If, after all, we are brothers and sisters then we gladly share what our Father has provided for us. Paul said,

"Remember to help one another." When times get difficult, remember to help one another.

III. REJOICE

The third principle is found in verse four. "REJOICE no matter what happens." It does not matter what happens to the dollar. What matters is what happens to you. How are you going to react? Are you going to believe what the Word says: Everything is possible if you believe. And if you believe, standing fast, helping one another, then you can learn to rejoice no matter what happens.

Recently a lady shared this story with me. "As I went to the grocery store a few days ago, I was extremely depressed because I knew everything was going to be higher. 'Higher and Higher' - that's the theme of the week. And as I walked in, sure enough," she said, "I was not disappointed. Everything was higher. Just as I expected. As I pushed the cart throughout the store, I was feeling very sorry for myself." She said to herself, "I don't know how I'm going to feed my family. I can't even afford to buy beans anymore."

The people who are always hurt the worst by financially tough times are the poor. The staple products which have been their mainstay in times past are now also too expensive to purchase. It is a serious problem. We are going to have to help each other.

This lady said, "All of a sudden, I looked around the aisle and there came a lady who had a little child with her which was crippled and was not able to walk straight." The lady said, "I wanted to fall on my knees right there and ask God to forgive my grumbling because at home all my children are healthy and strong." I said, "God, forgive me for complaining about something as insignificant as the price of food and help me learn to rejoice." The psalmist David said, "I have never seen the righteous begging bread." It does not matter what happens, God's children are not going to starve. We are learning to share, and we are learning to pull together. God is taking care of us.

The fact is - if we learn to stand in the Lord and help one another and we learn to rejoice, we are already on the road to having every need met.

IV. BE MODERATE

The fourth principle is found in verse five, "LET YOUR MODERATION BE KNOWN TO ALL MEN." That means to be balanced in everything that you do, including your finances. You do not need to be involved in reckless spending, but must be sure that at this time, more than ever before, you are considering purchasing only things which are truly needed. I am sharing this with you after hours of prayer. I am not an economist. I do not claim to be, but I do believe that the Spirit is telling me to speak the following.

The Word of God has an answer for every principle of life. Centuries ago God was able to give us an answer for the economic problems we face today through the writings of Paul. He said that everything you do, do in moderation. Do you know what that means? It means to be balanced. Use some good wisdom. Do not live the way your neighbors live, who never pray, who never seek God. Do not follow the ungodly counsel of the world, but stay on your knees until God tells you what to buy, and He will even tell you when to buy it.

God will give you an inner thought. Recently I needed a certain item. It was a need - not a luxury. I was skimming the newspaper, there was the item. A price was not listed, but I had the thought to call and check on the price. It was exactly what I needed at a reasonable price.

God is watching over you even at this moment. Seek God in every financial decision.

V. DO NOT WORRY

The fifth principle concerns our mental outlook. REFUSE TO WORRY. Verse six says, "Be careful for nothing." Do not be anxious about the circumstances. I repeat, refuse to worry. A survey by the American Medical Association revealed that 90% of the people who worry, worry about things that don't take place 87% of the time. Most of the time we waste our energy worrying about what might happen and it never happens.

I want to help you to learn to refuse to worry even when everything around you looks dim. Keep your eyes looking up. As I was driving to church recently on a Sunday morning, I was praising the Lord for the rain. I looked out and the clouds covered the whole sky except for one small hole. And through that hole the sun was just shining down. I thought to myself, "When all the financial clouds seem to be closing in around us and our skies are covered with problems, there is always going to be the sunlight of Jesus shining through."

Worry is so pointless. Worry always assumes the worse in any situation. Worry is a huge energy drain.

Worry tends to be about the past or the future. Can you relive the past? Can you foretell the future? Absolutely not!

I like the way English writer, Thomas Carlisle, puts it: "When you cannot see what is dimly in the future, do what is clearly at hand."

Jesus spoke similar words - "Every day has enough problems of its own. Live one day at a time." One day is enough!

VI. THINK POSITIVELY

Principle number six is to THINK POSITIVELY. Verse 8 says, "To think on honest, pure, lovely things of a good report." Think on these things. You cannot listen to the television for hours each day, day in and day out, and think positive God-kind of thoughts. You cannot read the junk that the world puts out on the literature stand and keep on thinking positive God kind of thoughts. Much of what we hear on television and read in the newspapers is negative. Wisdom would require you to limit your exposure to such negativism.

I am not suggesting that you never listen to the news to be informed. I am suggesting that you limit the amount of intake of negative information.

We are losing the art of meditation. Just being quiet to think, to muse, to meditate is a frightening idea for most people.

I thoroughly enjoy going to our House of Prayer at Hillcrest Church in Dallas. There in the quiet beauty of that room, I can think about God. The meditation on God's Word produces life - inner energy and creativity.

I love to mediate on Joshua 1:8, which states:

> *Do not let this Book of the Law depart from your mouth; meditate on it day and night, so that you may be careful to do everything written in it. Then you will be prosperous and successful.*

Think about it!

We are living in an hour when we cannot afford the luxury of being filled with the junk of this world. We need to be very perceptive of the material our eyes see. We need to be very selective with what we allow our ears to hear. We must be very, very careful, because when our minds are full of the garbage of the world, we cannot think on the God kind of things.

> *Whatever is pure and honest and true and lovely and of a good report think on these things. If there be any virtue or if there be any praise, think on these things.*
>
> Philippians 4:8 (Paraphrased)

VII. LEARN TO BE CONTENT

Principle number 7: LEARN TO BE CONTENT, in whatever state you are in. The apostle Paul said, "I have lived in luxury. I have lived in hunger. I have learned how to be content." I know very few people in America today who have learned how to be content. You know what one of our problems is? We are always chasing the pot of gold at the end of the rainbow. There is nothing wrong with achievement. There is nothing wrong with progress, and there is nothing wrong with wanting to provide better for your family. If, however, you are driven by a spirit of greed, that is wrong. Learn to be content in whatever state you are in. Whatever condition you are in, learn to be content.

My dear, old grandmother, I can see her now. She only weighed about 90 pounds dripping wet. Though she was very poor, she was a sweet little lady who loved the Lord. My cousin and I used to spend the summer with her, and in the evening she would say, "Boys, come in. Let's go through the motions again." What she meant by that was: there was not a whole lot to eat, but we would share what she had and enjoy being together. I learned from my dear grandmother that whatever was on the table, she always bowed her head and said, "God we thank you for this food you have provided."

Some of you may be like a story I heard about Peter Marshall who came home for his dinner one evening when he was the chaplain of the United States Congress. His wife, Catherine, had refrigerator-clean-out-day. He sat down and said, "Catherine, I believe you are going to have to pray over this tonight." Well, sometimes we complain about the refrigerator-clean-out-days, but we need to learn to be content with whatever is set before us.

VIII. COMMIT EVERYTHING TO GOD

The eighth principle is probably the most important one of all. It is to COMMIT EVERY NEED TO GOD, because verse 19 says, "But my God shall supply all your need according to his riches in glory by Christ Jesus." Jesus said, "Live one day at a time." Did you know that Jesus said that? He told us, "Sufficient unto the day is the evil thereof." There is enough trouble today not to worry about tomorrow. So live one day at a time. Jesus also said, "Lay up for yourself treasure in Heaven where moth and rust cannot get to it and thieves cannot steal, because where your heart is, that is where your treasure is going to be" (paraphrased).

The word "commit" is interesting. It literally means "to hand over." As you "hand over" your life, family, job, possessions to God, He becomes a partner in managing life with you. God is an excellent partner!

He knows how to supply "your need," not necessarily "your want." Although, I must quickly add that God is an abundant God who provides even more than our needs.

Not long ago, I had an amazing experience. I was preaching at the great Bethesda Church in Sterling Heights, Michigan. After the service, and attractive African-American couple approached me. The lady smiled, "You don't remember me, do you?" I looked. "Could it be?" - my mind raced. It was.

"Stella?" I said questioningly. "Yes," she said and gave me a big hug. "Meet my husband, Pastor Sheats."

Some twenty years earlier I was knocking on doors in the worst housing project in Lubbock, Texas, inviting people to Trinity Church where I pastored.

A lady opened the door of a run-down apartment. I introduced myself. She said rather quickly, "I know you, I watch you on television." She said, "I know you will believe what happened to me last week." She then told me a remarkable story of God sending "an angel" (Stella's words) to bring her and her children food when the cabinets were empty.

Now twenty years later, she stood before me again. She told me how God had blessed her. Her children were grown and doing well. God had given her a godly husband (her first husband deserted her). She said with a twinkle in her eyes "Pastor Sheats, I learned so much from you at Trinity Church. Then you moved to Dallas. Today, here in Detroit, I see you again. All I can say is that God's mercy is everlasting. He has provided well for me."

Thanks be to God! Stella learned to commit everything to God.

CHAPTER 7

REACTIONS

One of the most significant chapters in the entire book of Acts is a chapter that deals with the persecution of the early church (chapter 8). A great deal of persecution broke out as a result of the death of Stephen. Present at that stoning was a young man between the ages of twenty and twenty-five whose name was Saul. He was filled with a tremendous amount of hatred for the early church; his desire was to do his best to destroy the church.

If you do not understand this, then you need to remember that Jesus Himself said that satan comes to "steal, to kill, and to destroy" (John 10:10). I literally believe that is the purpose of satan. Every time I counsel with someone who has tried to commit suicide, I am made to believe more than ever before that it is satan's work to try to destroy the creation of God.

But, I remind you that Jesus is more powerful than all the powers of satan. For the Bible says,

> *Greater is He that is within you than he that is in the world.*
> I John 4:4

The power of Jesus can supersede and combat the power of satan. That is good news, and I am excited about that. However, satan was trying to destroy the early Church and persecution began to break out.

I. PERSECUTION PRODUCES PAIN.

First, PERSECUTION PRODUCES PAIN. When you are being persecuted, you will react with either physical or emotional pain. It is satan's goal to come against us, persecute us, and destroy us. My friends, it is not the persecution that is important - it is our reaction to that persecution. Once and for all, you must understand if you are a born-again child of God, and you have committed yourself to Jesus Christ, you will have some opposition. If you never have any opposition, if you are never treated in an unchristian manner then something may be lacking in your relationship to the Lord. The apostle John said,

> *Marvel not my brethren if the world hate you.*
>
> I John 3:13

and Jesus Himself said,

> *If the world hate you, ye know that it hated me before it hated you.*
>
> John 15:18

We ought never to be shocked at any treatment we receive from anyone. I know people who are out of church today because they said, "Someone in the church was not fair with me." My friend, every person reading this has committed sin. Every person in every congregation has made errors. All of us have gone astray and missed God from time to time. There are many times that our actions have been wrong. We should not be shocked when the actions of a Christian are not what they should be. We still live in a carnal world.

What I am trying to say to you is this: do not get your mind and your eyes on people, on churches, on preachers. Keep your eyes on Jesus Christ, Who is the author and the finisher of all your faith. He is the Lord of Lords and the King of Kings. He is the One Who brings victory and power and strength. He is the One Who brings triumphant joy.

When you encounter a person whose actions are not what they should be, and you are hurt, remember to pray for that person. We all need to ask ourselves this question. Are we really reacting the way Jesus wants us to react? Remember, persecution produces pain.

Early in life I experienced the pain of persecution. My religious upbringing was very legalistic. I was told "we do not go to movies, or dance, or go to school parties." This "separation doctrine" was pounded into my brain. Therefore, even by the first grade I was thoroughly indoctrinated with all the "do not's" of our religion.

In the first grade, one day it was raining. The teacher said, "We will get our exercise by dancing." I can still remember the sheer panic that gripped my heart. I sat there.

When I did not get in the circle the teacher asked why. I told her. The other children snickered. I was humiliated. The snickering turned into name-calling on the play grounds the next day. I felt the pain of persecution.

Yet, today, I know God used that painful persecution to build strength in my inner man. I learned to stand alone.

Persecution produces pain. Persecution, however, produces progress.

II. PERSECUTION PRODUCES PROGRESS

Now let us go a step further. Secondly, PERSECUTION PRODUCES PROGRESS. It is when we are persecuted that we begin to grow spiritually. It is when people put us down that we begin to rise up. It is when everything is not going exactly right that God begins to give us strength.

You see, our reactions to life reveal our true nature. The prophet Jeremiah said, "The heart is deceitful above all things and desperately wicked." Isaiah said, "All we like sheep have gone astray, we have turned everyone to his own way. The Lord hath laid on him the iniquity of us all." God says that we must see our basic nature as sinful, deceitful, and selfish. For indeed, we are a self-centered people. We want our own way. This is revealed through our reactions. Remember our reactions to life reveal our true nature (character).

Have you ever had a conflict within your home where someone behaved with a negative or critical spirit? Then the reactions were condemnation and self-pity? It is a vicious cycle. The husband says, "I am going to change when you change." The wife says, "I am going to change when you change." And no one changes. It is a stalemate, a deadlock and no one is better off. I repeat, it is not the circumstances of your life which control you - it is your reactions to those circumstances which control you!

J. Allan Peterson of Family Life Crusades, Denver, gives this illustration. Take a tea bag and drop it into a cup of hot water. As we look at it, we see the brown color begin to ooze out of this little tea bag and color all the water. The hot water simply brought out what was already in the tea bag. We have to face the reality of life. How many times have you been in hot water with your husband or your children. Like the dark brown color that comes from the tea bag, something unchristian shows up in our reactions. We cannot blame someone else for putting that into us. The truth is that he or she merely brought out what was already inside of us.

I have thought about "the tea bag illustration" much the last days. My wife and I are in England for a working vacation. We have been drinking a lot of tea while I have been rewriting and polishing this manuscript.

I have observed something about tea. The hotter the water, the quicker the tea becomes dark. What an illustration. When we're in "real hot water," how quickly the worse in us comes out. We must guard our hearts and make certain that when tough times come, when persecution comes, that we do not over-react. We must concentrate on making progress in tough times, not in simply reacting from the dark side of our hearts. Remember, reactions to life can be controlled by a calm heart guided by the Holy Spirit.

Let us look in the Living Bible at what Jesus says about our reactions. Remember, persecution produces pain, but hopefully persecution will also produce progress. Especially when we look on the inside of ourselves.

> *And then He added, it is the thought life that pollutes. For from within, out of men's hearts, come evil thoughts of lust, theft, murder, adultery, wanting what belongs to others, wickedness, deceit, lewdness, envy, slander, pride, and all other folly. All these vile things come from within; they are what pollute you and make you unfit for God.*
>
> Mark 7:20-23

When you, in a moment's time, lose your temper, it is because you have a temper on the inside that is ready to be lost. It is already there. When you in a moment's time, can react very negatively and criticize a brother or a sister, it is because ill will is already on the inside of you. When I say persecution produces progress, it is because it causes us to look on the inside and say, "Heavenly Father, cleanse me. Put the magnifying glass on my soul, and point out the areas where I am reacting in an unchristian way."

It is no wonder that some people in the world do not want to be saved, the way they see church people reacting to the situations of life. Just think for a minute. You are very busy. You are very rushed. You are trying to make an appointment. You run out of gas. How many of us say, "Oh hallelujah, this is wonderful; I am out of gas and I am already ten minutes late. What a wonderful opportunity to demonstrate positive reactions?" Most of us get out and mumble, grumble, spit and spew.

Persecution is one of the ways to grow up spiritually. When things come against you, you may not be happy about them. However, if you can possess a reaction that is positive, you are making progress. Think prayerfully about this truth!

III. PERSECUTION PRODUCES PRAISE.

Not only does persecution produce pain, and out of the pain comes progress, but PERSECUTION PRODUCES PRAISE. Acts 8 tells us when this great persecution broke out, the Christians were spread everywhere from Jerusalem. I suggest that if the persecution had never come, perhaps the early Christians would never have left Jerusalem. Things were just too good there. The Spirit was touching lives, people were being healed. It was beautiful and wonderful. The persecution, however, drove them out. One of the deacons, Philip, went to Samaria and began to preach. There demon-possessed people with all kinds of mental and physical disorders were healed by the power of Jesus. And verse 8 of Acts 8 says, "There was great joy in the city."

Why? Because persecution produced praise unto God. Oh, How many times have you been able to praise the Lord in the midst of your problems? Were you able to rejoice for the work God was doing even through your difficulties and the things satan brought against you?

I hope everyone will read this next statement very carefully. I hope that every teenager can get this statement and tuck it away in his mind for the years ahead. Here it is. Nothing in this world can hurt you, except your own reactions. It is not the problem you have right now which is causing you to be nervous and full of anxiety. It is your reaction to that problem. I repeat, nothing in this world can hurt you, except your reactions.

I have ached on the inside many times as I have stood at the bedside of people in the church I pastor. People who were going through great emotional disturbances. People in pain. People suffering because of the loss of loved ones. People in trouble because they failed and missed God's will. I have stood there and have agonized on the inside many times. But through it all, I have come to believe without any doubt that we can stand secure on the Word of God. Romans 8:28 says, "We know that all things work together for good to them that love God, to them who are called according to His purpose."

I did not say that everything that happens to you is good. Everything that happens to you is not good. But God can take even the most evil, self-degrading situation and bring peace and joy. That is why I say persecution can produce praise. As you grow up spiritually, you can praise the Lord in the difficulties of life. It's not easy to do, but we can learn to do it.

I remember standing beside the bedside of a lady who had had many surgeries. She was about to have another operation, and I said to her, "You have certainly had more than your fair share of suffering. But I can tell you one thing, this operation cannot hurt you." She said, "I do not understand, pastor, what do you mean?" Then I looked at her and said, "Oh, I realize it will hurt physically, but this operation cannot harm your inner self if you refuse to become bitter. If you stay sweet in your spirit, this operation cannot hurt you." It is not your circumstances, it is your reactions to those circumstances that will either make you or break you. The woman heard and successfully recovered.

Did Helen Keller give in to the hurt of being blind? Did Beethoven quit writing symphonic orchestrations because he became deaf? Did Thomas Edison refuse to begin because he had only three months of formal education? Did Job give up when every conceivable wrong had happened to his household and even his wife said, "Curse God and die."? Did Abraham Lincoln expect failure because he was raised in abject poverty? Do you think John the Apostle was hurt when he was sentenced to the Isle of Patmos to be in exile, to be in prison? No, my friend. He just plugged into the Heavenly hotline, and God gave him the Book of Revelation.

It is up to you! You can react to your circumstances in any manner you choose. The Bible says in I Thessalonians, "See that you never render evil for evil." The word "see" means "to understand, to visualize" to see yourself never rendering evil for evil. Persecution comes and persecution produces pain. Then when we start to hurt on the inside, we begin to make progress. When we begin to make progress, we are growing up and we can realize that we can praise God in all the ways of our life.

I want to talk to you out of my heart for just a moment. Perhaps you are saying, "Pastor Sheats, you do not understand. I am not responsible for my reactions. Life has done me dirty, and I have been given a raw deal. I am not to blame." You may not be responsible for the circumstances of your life, but you are responsible for your reactions to those circumstances. Pardon the vernacular terminology, but it is a bunch of garbage when a person says, "I could not do anything about the way I reacted." Yes, my friend, you always have the choice of the way you are going to react.

I have a little sign by the telephone in my office. It is one sentence. It says, "YOU CAN CHANGE YOUR MOODS LIKE YOU CHANGE YOUR CLOTHES." I believe that. I believe we have given most Americans the greatest cop-out in the world when we have said to them, "There is nothing you could have done about the situation." I realize that sometimes people are temporarily insane. I would not argue that. But I also believe that about 99% of the time most people are just throwing temper tantrums to get their own way. They have never grown up into mature persons.

I write this to you in love. It is not your circumstances in life, it is not whether you are rich or poor, or white or brown or black. None of those things can cause you to succeed or fail. It is your reactions to those circumstances of life that will make you or break you.

You say, "Pastor Sheats, what am I going to do? My reactions have not been very Christian lately." If your reactions have not been very Christian, then there is only one thing for you to do. Confess them as a sin unto God. Be forgiven. Be delivered. Move on up to higher ground. "If we confess our sins, he is faithful and just to forgive us of our sins, and to cleanse us from all unrighteousness" (John 1:9). The apostle Paul said, "I am crucified with Christ, nevertheless I live, yet not I, but Christ lives in me" (Galatians 2:20). If your reactions are not what you want them to be, let Jesus live in you.

Teens, if you have trouble with mom and dad, and your reactions are nasty criticism, just say, "Jesus, change me on the inside, so I can react to mom and dad in a positive way." Parents, if your reaction to your children is to knock them across the head and tell them to shut up, just say, "Jesus, cleanse me, and bring a peace inside of me so that I can react in a positive way to my children."

Do not misunderstand me. I am not talking about Utopia. I know we are all going to make mistakes. I know we are all going to sin. I know we are all going to say things we should not say. I do believe, however, by the grace of God we can become stronger Christians, more mature Christians. Our reactions can be more Christlike. That is the goal. That is the challenge. How will you react?

CHAPTER 8

HOW TO TURN SORROW INTO JOY

The Spirit of the Lord God is upon me; because the Lord hath anointed me to preach good tidings unto the meek; he hath sent me to bind up the brokenhearted, to proclaim liberty to the captives, and the opening of the prison to them that are bound; to proclaim the acceptable year of the Lord, and the day of vengeance of our God; to comfort all that mourn; to appoint unto them that mourn in Zion, to give unto them beauty for ashes, the oil of joy for mourning, the garment of praise for the spirit of heaviness; that they might be called Trees of righteousness, The planting of the Lord, that he might be glorified.

Isaiah 61:1-3

This is a prophetic passage. It talks about the time when Jesus would come and what He would do. Isaiah said He would be anointed to preach; He would bring good tidings; He would bind up the brokenhearted, and bring liberty to those who are in captivity. He will open the prison to those that are bound.

What is your prison today? Where are you bound? Whatever it is, Jesus wants to set you free. Isaiah prophesied, some 800 years before the coming of Christ, that when Christ came He would proclaim liberty to those who were in captivity and he would bind up the brokenhearted. This passage is the first sermon that Jesus ever preached.

When Jesus began His public ministry in the little town of Nazareth, His home synagogue, He stood and read these words from Isaiah because He wanted all the people to know that this was truly why He had come.

I. BEAUTY FOR ASHES

Now, may I call your attention to verse three. Notice specifically that a divine exchange occurs when God comes into our lives. We exchange some negatives for some positives. Jesus, in speaking about His ministry, says that He will bring BEAUTY FOR ASHES. If you want to paraphrase it, try saying -

"He will bring forgiveness for remorse." As a pastor I have talked to people who at different times have said something like this to me. "I have committed such great sins. I have wronged God so much, I could never really have any joy." They come burdened down, tremendously remorseful about what they have done with their lives. They need to realize that God wants to take that sorrow and bring forgiveness - the opposite of remorse.

There is a point for remorse and a time for repentance. There is a time when we need to cleanse our heart, turn from our iniquities, and be pure before God. But after we do that, God believes that you mean business and instead of heaping condemnation upon you, He says, "Have some beauty, be forgiven."

It was a custom in the Old Testament to take ashes, literally, and pour them over your head when you were repenting for your sins. Do you remember the story when Jonah finally obeyed God and went to the town of Nineveh? As Jonah preached, the conviction of God settled upon the people, and they all sat down in the streets and heaped ashes upon their heads as a symbol of repentance and remorse. As a result, one hundred thousand people were converted. Incidentally, as far as I know, that is the greatest single revival in the history of mankind, for an entire city, from the mayor to the lowliest servant, repented. They took the ashes and symbolically poured them over themselves as a symbol of their remorse. The Bible goes on to say that after they did, great gladness filled the city. If you are walking around under the bondage of condemnation as though you were covered with ashes, you are not where God wants you to be. He wants to give us forgiveness in exchange for our repentant act.

In the Book of James the same word is used in the Greek language for "beauty" that was used in the Isaiah 61 in the Hebrew language.

> *Blessed is the man that endureth temptation, for when he is tried, he shall receive the crown of life.*
>
> James 1:12

"The crown of life" is translated "beauty" in Isaiah 61. So, the man who endures temptation shall receive "beauty" or "the crown of life" which the Lord has promised to them that love Him. In other words, when you come to Jesus, you repent of your sins, ask God to forgive you and set you free. He says, "It is done. Instead of ashes I am going to give you a crown of life." Most of the time folks think about the crown of life and say, "That is someday way off when we get to heaven." No, forgiveness - the crown of life - starts right now. I believe in this life God desires to surround His children with life. Life now!

The whole world is dying. People may be walking around, but they are dead on the inside. They have no life whatsoever within them. When Jesus comes in, He breaks the bondage; He snaps the chains of oppression; He liberates. All of a sudden you can stand up on the inside, and you can even stand up on the outside, and say, "World, where are you; I am ready to live because I am no longer under condemnation; I am no longer under guilt; I am no longer under this ash heap. I am standing tall crowned with the Glory of God, forgiven."

I get excited about this truth. I guarantee you, when you realize who you are, a child of God redeemed by the blood of Jesus, and when you begin to take your rightful place in the community of life, the society of humanity all around you is going to look and say, "Hey!

What is going on? What has happened to you?" Then you can smile and look them in the eye and tell them what happened. "I had an encounter with Jesus."

I met a man a few days ago and he said, "You know, you carry a lot of responsibility, but when I see you, you always seem to have a joy, you seem to have a peace." I said, "Why, not? The Prince of Peace lives inside of me." Do you believe that Jesus lives inside of you? Jesus said, "Well, I am going away and since I cannot literally be here beside you, I am going to send the Holy Spirit and He is going to be with you and He is going to dwell IN you." So you make a divine exchange. You come with your ashes, your condemnations, your remorse, your repentance; and in return, you receive glory, beauty, forgiveness, and a crown of righteousness. That is a pretty good exchange!

II. THE OIL OF JOY FOR MOURNING

Secondly, Isaiah prophesied when Jesus would come He would bring THE OIL OF JOY FOR MOURNING. Now, the word for "oil" in the Scriptures represents the Holy Spirit. You can see that in the Old and the New Testaments. For example, when they were going to anoint the King of Israel, they used oil, which was a symbol of the Holy Spirit. When we pray for people, we place a little portion of oil on their head as a symbol or a picture of the Holy Spirit, according to James, chapter five. The anointing with oil is always a picture of the Holy Spirit. Isaiah prophesied 800 years before Jesus came and said, "You are going to have the oil of joy instead of mourning." Do you know what He was saying? He was proclaiming that you would have the POWER of the Holy Spirit in your life. Many of you reading this have been too mournful. Some of you feel like there is no purpose in living. But when you begin to receive beauty for ashes, when you begin to receive the oil of joy, which is the power of the Holy Spirit, you are going to have a purpose for living in this world.

In I John 2:20 there is a powerful verse sometimes overlooked because it is not understood. Let me explain to you.

But ye have an unction from the Holy One.

I John 2:20

Some people think that the word "unction" only applies to the Roman Catholic Church because they administer what is called "Extreme Unction" when a person is near death. A practice not even introduced until the eighth century. Prior to that century, the anointing of oil was for healing, not preparation for death. But this Scripture is not talking about "Extreme Unction." This verse is talking about you, the believer, who has an unction. The word "unction," if you actually transliterate it, is the word "anointment." In the Greek it is the word "chrisma" which is an ointment that is a thick consistency which you could put on your head to give you a sweet fragrance. Now, think about that. You have been given a special anointment from the Holy One through the Holy Spirit, Who knows all things. This is one of the most powerful verses in the entire Bible. As a believer, you are anointed by the Holy Spirit.

You do not need to read what someone has written in a horoscope to tell you how to live. You do not need to go to some kind of book to try to figure out what you are going to do the next day. You only need to stay in tune with Jesus Who will anoint you with the Holy Spirit, Who will then give you guidance to understand the things that are going to happen. Look at that verse again. You have an unction, an anointing from the Holy One, and the result of that anointing is that you shall know all things. Do you get excited when you think about that? That means when the Holy Spirit comes upon us we have divine insight. The wisest people in all the world should be the people filled with God's Spirit.

Also, when you are filled with God's Spirit you have joy. What does the book of Romans say about the Kingdom of God? It says the Kingdom of God is righteousness, peace, and JOY in the Holy Spirit (Romans 14:17). Now, joy is not the same thing you feel when you get a new car. If you get a new car or you get something new around the house it makes you feel good and that is happiness. You feel good about it until about thirty days later when you get the bill in the mail - then you may not feel so good. But there is a period of happiness. On the other hand, there is a thing called joy. Joy is a peace inside no matter what happens. No matter what happens! You get that new car and your mother-in-law drives it off a cliff - you may not be too happy, but you can still keep your joy. You see, it is way down deep inside. Joy is something that is not superficial.

Almost all the commercials you see advertising products are superficial. You do this and you are going to get this much happiness. You try this fad and it will make you happy. One month it is one thing and the next month it is something else. A person on Madison Avenue in New York City sits there and is paid to come up with something new, that you will run out and try. The world runs out and tries it. The sense of ownership is short lived. Your heart yearns for something deeper, less superficial. Your heart longs for reality.

Reality comes with the power of the Holy Spirit and receiving the oil of joy that flows from the top of your head to the bottom of your feet. No matter what happens, you can stand up and say, "Thank you Jesus for the oil of the Holy Spirit. I no longer mourn; I no longer have to cry; I no longer have to live the way the world says I have to live. I can have peace whether I am in a mansion or whether I am in a shack, because I have the anointing of the oil of the Holy Spirit. It will take me through the hard times, and it will take me through the good times."

Oil was always used in the Old Testament when they had a festival. It was not used when they were having a time of repentance. Look at Psalm 45:7, speaking prophetically, once again of Jesus. This in a sense, however, is our promise.

> *Thou lovest righteousness, and hatest wickedness, therefore God, thy God, hath anointed thee with the oil of gladness above*

thy fellows.

Psalm 45:7

Now, I want you to zero in on that last phrase. This is talking about Jesus, that he is going to be anointed with the oil of gladness above all of His fellow men. If we are to be like Jesus, Philippians 2 says that we are to have the mind of Christ. If we are to have the mind of Christ and walk in His steps, then we should also have the oil of gladness above our fellows. That means everyone around you. That means that Christians should just stick out in a crowd.

It is time for Christians to stop taking the back seat. We need Christians in the White House. We need Christians in every major office in these United States of America. We need Christians on our city council and on our school board who can stand up and say, "I am covered by the oil of joy, so therefore I have gladness even above everyone else." You say, "Are you being egotistical or self-righteous?" I do not mean it that way. But I do believe that the Christians should have such gladness that everyone else will say, "I wish I had some of that."

Some people's idea of having a good time is going out and spending hard-earned money drinking liquor and having a party. Someone said to me recently, "How could you afford to buy that?" My reply was, "Man, all the things that the Lord has kept me from will really pay for a lot of things that you cannot afford." I am not going to tell you what you should be delivered from. The Holy Spirit can do that a whole lot better than I can. But let me share this truth: when you come to Jesus and receive the oil of the Holy Spirit, you do not need any other kind of liquid to run on. You can have beauty for ashes and the oil of joy for mourning. What do you want? Do you want ashes or forgiveness?

It is your decision. You have to decide.

You see, we need the Holy Spirit today, and I would like to share a letter with you which will show you more conclusively than anything that I could ever write, how this oil of joy takes the place of mourning.

Pastor Sheats,

I waited several weeks before I sent this letter. During this time I occasionally lost the joy of the Lord, but each time I found it again by sharing or witnessing what God has done for me.

Now, there is the real key. When you feel like your joy is leaving, you ignore your feelings and continue to tell people about the goodness of God. The more you talk about the goodness of God, all of a sudden your old machinery is going to get oiled up again.

I have been to three psychiatrists. These men who charge about two dollars a minute for their time did nothing for me except give me medicine to escape my problems. Most of the time the medicine did not help at all. When I finally had the courage, I called the church for counseling. The next day I was so hungry for the Word of God I didn't have time for any soap operas. I was watching every one of those things. I bought a cassette tape player and I thank God that I am a housewife, so that I can listen to the Word of God on tape. I'm still having a few problems, but I ask your prayers that my husband will be patient with me and I am growing.

That is a powerful letter. That person made a divine exchange - from sorrow to joy. They exchanged their mourning for the oil of joy. I am not saying that you will never have any more problems. However, if when you have problems, keep on shouting the good news saying, "The Lord is my strength. In whom shall I fear?" You will have power to do things that you never dreamed you could do before.

III. THE GARMENT OF PRAISE FOR THE SPIRIT OF HEAVINESS

The third thing that Isaiah prophesied about Jesus, and of course it is for us, is that we would have THE GARMENT OF PRAISE FOR THE

SPIRIT OF HEAVINESS. Do you know what the word, "heaviness" means in the Hebrew? The same word for "heaviness" in Isaiah is used in Psalm 42:3 referring to "putting out a lamp." When you have a heavy heart you feel like the lamp is out on the inside. Isn't that a descriptive way of saying it? I am going to exchange my feeling of "the lamp going out on the inside of me" for a garment of praise, and the word "garment" literally means "covering." I'm going to be covered all over with praise.

> *I will bless the Lord at all times: his praise shall continually be in my mouth. My soul shall make her boast in the Lord; the humble shall hear thereof, and be glad. O magnify the Lord with me, and let us exalt his name together.*
>
> Psalm 34:1-3

Let those words sink into your heart. "I will bless the Lord at all times. His praise shall continually be in my mouth." I have come to the conclusion in counseling with hundreds and hundreds of people that many times individuals get into a habit of heaviness. They get into the habit of feeling bad. They get into the habit of saying, "I am discouraged." By the same token, you can get into the habit of praising the Lord. Now, it takes some time to develop the habit of heaviness. Some of you have it. It is also going to take some time to develop the habit of praise. But the habit of praise will cover like a garment the habit of heaviness. Instead of feeling like your light is going to go out, you are going to feel like you are going to explode because praise is going to cover your feelings of heaviness and depression.

When you start getting discouraged, when you start getting depressed, when you start getting troubled, the very first thing to do, is start forcing yourself to praise the Lord with your lips. Thank God with your mouth; praise Him for being God; praise Him for being the Lord. You may say, "That is being hypocritical." No, it is not. It is not hypocritical, because you know it is true and the pattern works. If you will begin to praise the Lord, then the old feelings of heaviness are going to be stripped away, and the new garment of praise is just going to fall all over you.

And what's going to happen now? Let's go back to Isaiah 61. Isaiah says that when the Lord comes, He is going to anoint us; He is going to give us beauty for ashes; He is going to give us the garment of praise for the spirit of heaviness or depression. Isaiah 61:3 says that you might be called the trees of righteousness. Literally, the word used for "trees" is "oaks" - OAKS. You know what an oak tree is. It is one of the slowest growing trees there is, but it is also about the most sturdy tree there is. You are going to be called the oaks of righteousness, the planting of the Lord. That you might be glorified? No! That He might be glorified!

Oak trees are durable. I have seen historic homes in England where the beams were made of oak. The lecturer emphasized - "oak beams." Why? Oak is solid. Oak is durable. Oak lasts.

Do you get it? God wants to make you like an oak tree - so that you may bring glory to His name through your dependable character.

CHAPTER 9

SUFFERING: THE COMMON DENOMINATOR

But and if ye suffer for righteousness sake, happy are ye: and be not afraid of their terror, neither be troubled; But sanctify the Lord God in your hearts: and be ready always to give an answer to every man that asketh you a reason of the hope that is in you with meekness and fear: Having a good conscience that, whereas they speak evil of you, as of evildoers, they may be ashamed that falsely accuse your good conversation in Christ.
For it is better, if the will of God be so, that ye suffer for well doing, than of evil doing. For Christ also hath once suffered for sins, the just for the unjust, that he might bring us to God, being put to death in the flesh, but quickened by the Spirit.

I Peter 3:14-18

Forasmuch then as Christ hath suffered for us in the flesh, arm yourselves likewise with the same mind: for he that hath suffered in the flesh hath ceased from sin; That he no longer should live the rest of his time in the flesh to be lusts of men, but to the will of God. Beloved, think it not strange concerning the fiery trial which is to try you, as though some strange thing happened unto you. But rejoice inasmuch as ye are partakers of Christ's sufferings; that, when his glory shall be revealed, ye

may be glad also with exceeding joy.
If you be reproached for the name of Christ, happy are ye; for the Spirit of Glory and of God resteth upon you; on their part he is evil spoken of, but on your part he is glorified.
But let none of you suffer as a murderer, or as a thief, or as an evildoer, or as a busybody in other men's matters.
Yet if any man suffer as a Christian, let him not be ashamed; but let him glorify God on this behalf. For the time is come that judgment must begin at the house of God: and if it first begin at us, what shall the end be of them that obey not the gospel of God? And if the righteous scarcely be saved, where shall the ungodly and the sinner appear?
Wherefore, let them that suffer according to the will of God commit the keeping of their souls to him in well doing, as unto a faithful Creator.

I Peter 4:1, 2, 12-19

In many ways today, I feel like I am suffering on the inside. I suffer at the loss of brothers and sisters, gone to be with our Lord. I suffer because literally millions of Christians are going through tremendous persecution at this hour. As the Word of God says in I Corinthians 12, we suffer with those who suffer and rejoice with those who rejoice. I have come to the conclusion that suffering is part of all men's lives. There are some things in life which are common denominators of life, they are the common equalizers. All men have a birth; all men have a death. These are common denominators, and I am convinced that all men at some point in their lives experience suffering which also becomes a factor for all people. And so it is very understandable when we read of the people of God crying out as they did under the Egyptian Pharaoh's hard and heavy hand. "Oh, God, how long shall we suffer? How long shall we have to face the suffering issues of this life?"

Some men have financial reverses; they suffer. Some people have marriage problems; they suffer. Some people have the confidence of a friend broken and they suffer. But why? That seems to be the single question that comes down through all of the centuries. Why must man suffer? Well, I suppose one could oversimplify the answer and say, "Man suffers because of sin." And really, that is a pretty honest answer. If you want to get right down to the heart of the matter immediately, that really is the answer. Man suffers because of the sin of man.

"Well," you say, "what about the righteous? Why is it then that the righteous suffer?" Jesus tells us in Matthew chapter 6, that the rain comes upon the righteous and the unrighteous and the sunshine comes upon the righteous and the unrighteous. Peter, in the passage we began with, says at times it is the will of God to suffer. I was amazed at how many times Peter talks about the will of God in connection with suffering. Now, it is important at this point that we not be confused. He said if we suffer for the name of Christ, we are to rejoice, but we are not to be participants in evildoing. We are not to suffer because we have been a murderer, a thief, or a busybody. If you are suffering because of those kinds of things, then your suffering will not bring glory to God. Many people who are trying to serve Christ get involved in sinful living and evildoing. They become involved in gossiping and criticizing a brother or a sister, and they suffer because of it and then they ask God why they suffer.

There are times when we bring suffering on ourselves. I have made some bad decisions in my life, and I am sure I am not alone in that statement. I have suffered at times for poor judgment, but was that God's fault? In retrospect, I began to look and see that I had not even consulted the Father before making those bad decisions. You say, but what about the person who does seek God? What about the person who really is trying to live in a right relationship with God and they suffer? How do you explain that?

I would like to offer you some suggestions I believe the Holy Spirit has given me through the years in trying to find answers to encourage people and help them. However, I do not believe we are ever going to cover the issue totally in this life. Some questions will not be answered until we see Jesus face to face. Suffering is one.

I. SUFFERING PURIFIES THE SPIRIT.

I think there are times we suffer because SUFFERING PURIFIES THE SPIRIT. Notice how these admonitions were written. Peter uses the word "beloved." Did you know that both Peter and John only use the word "beloved" when they are speaking to the saints? "Beloved, (you saints) think it not strange concerning the fiery trial which is to try you, as though some strange thing happened to you." Peter was saying, "Do not think something strange is going on if you have a trial or a suffering, but rejoice inasmuch as you are partakers of Christ's suffering."

In another place Peter speaks of the trial where we come forth as pure gold. The jeweler takes the flame and heats the metal until the impurities float aside and only the gold is left. It is the teaching of the apostle Peter that suffering and trials come our way to aid in purifying the spirit. They are to aid in allowing your spirit to mature in the things of God. Although all of us have suffered, most of us have never known true suffering for the sake of the gospel. I think of suffering such as Watchman Nee knew, who for many years before his death was imprisoned in China because of his faith. That great man of God, who has written so many instructional insights of the body of Christ, suffered. Why did he suffer? Because when the Communists took over China in the late 1940's he said, "I will serve my God." But the suffering purified his spirit to the extent that he was able to record insights into the Scripture that most of us have not known. Suffering purifies and cleanses the spirit.

II. SUFFERING CORRECTS THE SOUL.

Secondly, I believe SUFFERING CORRECTS THE SOUL.

For the time is come that judgment must begin at the house of

God: and if it first begin with us at shall the end be of them that obey not the gospel of God? And if the righteous scarcely be saved where shall the ungodly and the sinner appear? Wherefore, let them that suffer according to the will of God commit the keeping of their souls to him in well doing as unto a faithful Creator.

I Peter 4:17-19

Suffering corrects the soul. Let's define the word "soul."

When you see the word "soul" or the word "heart," if you will just put in parentheses "the center of all rational and emotional decisions" you will have a better understanding of the Scriptures. So verse 19 would read like this: "Wherefore let them that suffer according to the will of God (evidently there are times when it is God's will for us to suffer) commit the keeping of their souls (the center of all rational and emotional decisions) to him in well doing."

Now, the problem that so often happens when people suffer is that they do not commit their soul unto God. They begin to take charge of "the center of all rational and emotional decisions." They begin to panic; they get upset, nervous, and jittery. Then they say, "God, why me? What are you doing to me? I'm going to run this thing because I believe I can do a better job than you are doing." They then take charge of the "center of rational and emotional decisions" and the result is they begin to make still more wrong rational and emotional decisions.

If, however, we will commit our souls to God when suffering comes, we can have our spirit cleansed and our souls corrected. When we are corrected, our thinking is given right direction and our decisions are made from the right perspective. You know, it is so easy to think that we have arrived. It is so nice for us to look around and say, "Look at me. Look at what I have done." Suffering tends to temper pride.

From time to time I have seen different personalities, perhaps on television, sometimes personally, after they have experienced defeat, and

I am always impressed with a humility in that person that I had never seen before. I have come to the conclusion that whenever people suffer, for whatever the reason might be, it is a humbling experience. As I watch people who go through suffering in life, I see their souls corrected. They are humbled and their arrogance seems to go away. God does that to allow us to grow, to allow our spirits to be cleansed and our souls to be corrected.

III. SUFFERING JOINS THE SUFFERER TO THE BODY.

Thirdly, I believe that SUFFERING JOINS THE SUFFERER TO THE BODY. Now, I do not mean the physical body, but the body of Christ. Suffering cleanses the spirit, it corrects the soul, and it connects you with the body of Christ. If you never suffered, if you have never had setbacks, if you never had any difficulties, how could you possibly understand when a brother or sister experiences problems.

Now, I know what I am saying may be considered controversial by some, because there is a doctrine or theology prevalent today which says the Christian need never suffer; the saints of God are the conquerors. I believe that, but I also must tell you I know what we say with our mouth is not always what we are believing in our spirit. You can say a thousand times with your mouth that everything is just rosy and perfect, but if you do not have a heart that has been regenerated and changed by the power of the Holy Spirit, all of your verbalization is just hot air. And this is the part that is sometime overlooked in the teaching of "What you confess with your mouth..." We must also "believe in our heart."

We must confess with our mouth the things of God; we must confess with our mouth the praises of God. We must also believe and teach that the heart of man must be changed. After our heart is changed, when we have a time of suffering, do we give up and say that the Word of God is not true? Or do we continue to press through the maze of life, the sufferings, trials, and problems that face us until we come into a deeper understanding of what life is all about. We should go aside and say, "What is God trying to teach me? What is God trying to say to me?"

> *The Spirit itself beareth witness with our spirit, that we are the children of God, And if children, then heirs; heirs of God, and joint-heirs with Christ, if so be that we suffer with him, that we may be also glorified together.*
> Romans 8:16, 17

This passage does not seem to say that suffering is an option. It seems to say that suffering is a necessity in order to be glorified with Him. It does not seem to indicate that suffering is something you can take or leave. IT SEEMS TO SAY SUFFERING IS A NECESSITY FOR GLORIFICATION.

We all like to read about glorification. We all love to hear about sitting in heavenly places and walking down the streets of gold. I had much rather study those passages in the Bible than the one I am sharing with you now, but the Word of God tells us we are going to suffer with Jesus that we may be glorified with Jesus.

> *For I reckon that the sufferings of this present time are not worthy to be compared with the glory which shall be revealed in us.*
> Romans 8:18

Some people say we are going to get all the glory revealed within us in this life. Please, do not ever accept that, because it is not biblically accurate. We are going to continue to be revealed in the glory of God in this life, but there are some things that are only going to be revealed to us when we see Jesus face to face. If anyone tells you, "You can understand everything now," they are not facing the issues. I repeat, you cannot understand everything about life. I serve God not because I understand everything about life, but because I do not understand everything about life. Therefore, I submit unto His ultimate will.

There is one thing I have been learning the last few years, and it is this. The final test of true spiritual maturity is whether or not you will accept the sovereignty of God as much when things are going bad as you do when things are going good. I have seen many people drop by the wayside when they experienced suffering. That is a heavy burden to me, my friend, because at the moment of suffering our lives should become stronger than ever before. Through our suffering our spirits are being cleansed, our souls are being corrected, and our bodies are being joined to the body of Christ. If you and I suffer, we are connected together in the body of Christ. This is the reason why Jesus suffered on the cross. He bore that suffering so that we could have life and be joined to Him as joint-heirs and to each other as fellow pilgrims.

When I speak of a "heavy burden" that I carry when a godly person turns away from God in the hour of suffering, I choose the words carefully. Pastoring is stressful work. Trying to keep a flock of people together is demanding. Then the burden of keeping people from casting aside their confidence in God when tough times come - it is a big challenge.

Phillip Yancey did the body of Christ a great service when he wrote, Disappointment With God. People—good, godly people—have disappointments in life. We all suffer.

It is easy to blame God. It is easy to say "why go to church" when the bottom falls out of life. Yet, in the hour of suffering, we need each other more than ever. The body of Christ is designed by God to function best under pressure. Jesus came through the suffering of the cross in order to help us when our "cross of suffering" comes.

Also, through His suffering, He was made able to understand our feelings and needs when we suffer. I made a statement in a sermon once that was challenged by a teenager. And I might insert here that I appreciate any teenager or any person questioning a teacher because they are interested, listening and desiring to learn. I had said that Jesus Christ understands every suffering of man. After the service the teenager said, "How could Jesus understand divorce?" That was a very perceptive question. The Lord immediately gave me an answer for that young person. Divorce is alienation and loneliness, and Jesus Christ experienced all of that on the cross. He experienced alienation from his own Father; God turned His back on Him. Jesus: "My God, my God, Why have you forsaken me?" I still believe that Jesus Christ understands every suffering of mankind.

A Christian lady slapped her hand on my desk one day in an absolute rage. Her nine year old son had been hit by a truck. He died.

"Where was God when my son died?", she demanded. I looked at her eyes. They were hurting. The etchings around her eyes seemed to scream at me. I did not have an answer.

I sat quiet for a few minutes. She waited. I was praying silently in my heart. "Oh, God, help me. This dear lady needs help."

Then the answer came. I looked at her with deep compassion and said, "Where was God when your son died? The same place He was when His Son died."

I have no idea where that thought cam from - except from the Holy Spirit. We prayed. We wept together. We hurt together. Today that godly lady still serves God. Jesus touched her and made her whole.

Therefore, I urge you to submit yourself to Jesus and know that when suffering or difficulty comes, you do not have to crawl into a hole and give up. In the Scripture which we have examined, we are admonished to rejoice in suffering. And that is the real test of victory in the Christian life.

I have seen families who have gone through the valley of the shadow of death. I have seen many families grow in spiritual gianthood through their testings, others have not grown as much, some not at all. The difference is whether the family chooses to rejoice in the sovereignty of God or question the sovereignty of God. I can assure you if you question the sovereignty of God, you will not rejoice; you will not have peace. You will become bitter, and you will be defeated as a person. When, however, you accept the sovereignty, holiness, and majesty of God; when you say, "God, I submit to You," then there is going to be a peace that will flow into you like you have never known before.

When the difficulties in life come, you can look up and keep your faith in Jesus because He is the only source of endurance in this world. Money, governments, and friends pass away, but JESUS CAME FORTH OUT OF THE GRAVE and He lives today. He is alive today. He is the only source of enduring life. LOOK TO HIM.

CHAPTER 10

HOW TO HANDLE FEAR

And it was told the king of Egypt that the people fled, and the heart of the Pharaoh and of his servants was turned against the people, and they said, Why have we done this, that we have let Israel go from serving us?

And he made ready his chariot, and took his people with him: And he took six hundred chosen chariots, and all the chariots of Egypt, and captains over every one of them.

And the Lord hardened the heart of Pharaoh king of Egypt, and he pursued after the children of Israel: and the children of Israel went out with a high hand. But the Egyptians pursued after them, all the horses and chariots of Pharaoh, and his horsemen, and his army, and overtook them encamping by the sea, beside Pihahiroth, before Baalzephon.

And when Pharaoh drew nigh, the children of Israel lifted up their eyes, and behold, the Egyptians marched after them; and they were sore afraid, and the children of Israel cried unto the Lord. And they said unto Moses, Because there were no graves in Egypt, hast thou taken us away to die in the wilderness? Wherefore, hast thou dealt thus with us, to carry us forth out of Egypt? Is not this the word that we did tell thee in Egypt, saying, Let us alone, that we may serve the Egyptians? For it had been better for us to serve the Egyptians, than that we should die in the wilderness.

And Moses said unto the people, Fear ye not, stand still, and see the salvation of the Lord, which he will show to you today: for the Egyptians whom ye have seen today, ye shall see them again no more forever. The Lord shall fight for you, and ye shall hold your peace.

And the Lord said unto Moses, Wherefore criest thou unto me? Speak unto the children of Israel, that they go forward: But lift thou up thy rod, and stretch out thine hand over the sea, and divide it: and the children of Israel shall go on dry ground through the midst of the sea. And I, behold, I will harden the hearts of the Egyptians, and they shall follow them: and I will get me honour upon Pharaoh, and upon all his host, upon his chariots, and upon his horsemen. And the Egyptians shall know that I am the Lord, when I have gotten me honour upon Pharaoh, upon his chariots, and upon his horsemen.

And the Lord said unto Moses, Stretch out thine hand over the sea, that the water may come again upon the Egyptians, upon their chariots, and upon their horsemen. And Moses stretched forth his hand over the sea, and the sea returned to his strength when the morning appeared; and the Egyptians fled against it; and the Lord overthrew the Egyptians in the midst of the sea. And the waters returned and covered the chariots, and the horsemen, and all the host of Pharaoh that came into the sea after them; There remained not so much as a one of them.

But the children of Israel walked upon dry land in the midst of the sea; and the waters were a wall unto them on their right hand, and on their left. Thus the Lord saved Israel that day out of the hand of the Egyptians; and Israel saw the Egyptians dead upon the sea shore. And Israel saw that great work which the Lord did upon the Egyptians: and the people feared the Lord, and believed the Lord, and his servant Moses.

Exodus 14:5-18, 26-31

There are seventy-five different fears listed in the dictionary; they are called phobias. Acrophobia, the fear of heights; claustrophobia, the fear of closed places; agoraphobia, the fear of open places; neophobia, the fear of something that is new; pathophobia, the fear of disease; photophobia, the fear of light; ergophobia, the fear of work (a lot of people have that); ereuthophobia, the fear of blushing (we could use a little bit more of that one). But to top them all, there is the fear, phobophobia, the fear of all things. I have known many people who have been afraid in life. I have met people like a teenage girl who said, "I am afraid I am going to be unpopular," and the businessman who said, "I am afraid of bankruptcy," or the possessive mother who said, "Pastor, I am afraid of losing my children's love and affection."

The teen had many problems. The businessman did go bankrupt. The mother did lose her children's love. Why? Fear is powerful. Fear produces results - negative results. Fear, however, properly dealt with can be turned into powerful energy for good.

There is a law of life, and it is stated in God's Word. Job made it perfectly clear when he said, "The thing I feared the most is come upon me." However, I have good news for you. Your greatest fear can become your greatest asset. I believe that with all my heart, because it is well defined in the story which we read. As the children of Israel looked back and saw the Egyptians approaching they were sore afraid - or in the Hebrew, they were "scared to death." Then they told Moses, "You just brought us out her to die," as the fear began to take control of them. Fear is like a cancer, just like the tentacle of satan himself, wrapping around your inner spirit and crushing the life within you. Yet God is not the Spirit of fear, but he is the Spirit of power and love and a sound mind.

There are five steps that you can utilize to turn your greatest fear into your greatest asset. I want you to be liberated from whatever is your greatest fear by turning that fear into your greatest asset. It can happen. It is going to happen.

I. FACE YOUR FEAR.

Whatever it is, you must learn to FACE YOUR FEAR. Moses said, "We are going to face the fact that the Egyptians are back there. We are not going to ignore it." Some people will advise you to just ignore your fear and it will go away, but it does not. It gets bigger. You see, you cannot ignore fear. Why? Because fear is sent by satan. Satan puts fear upon you, because he wants to crush you down and bury you underneath that fear. However, that is not the way of Christ. You see, when you face your fear you are facing satan, and praise God, he has already been defeated. So you are facing a defeated opponent. That gives you a distinct advantage. That gives you the ability to stand there and look him squarely in the eye and say, "Satan, although the circumstances may look discouraging. They may look like I am headed for defeat, but I want you to know I am a child of the King. I am washed in the blood of the Lamb and Jesus Christ is my Lord. He has conquered you, and His heel has smashed your head in the ground, and I am going to stand." FACE YOUR FEAR, because it is the enemy of your soul.

You say, "Well, you do not understand my fear." Perhaps yours is similar to a story I read in Bruce Larson's writings. He told about a skinny little boy with no flesh on his bones. Seeing all the other boys so strong and muscular, he decided he did not like being the runt. One day that little boy was reading a book and there was one sentence that leaped off the page. "Do the thing you fear the most and the death of that fear is certain." That got a hold of that little boy. "Do the thing you fear the most and the death of that fear is certain." So, he got involved in a physical building program; he began to eat right; he worked hard and when he was in high school, he found himself at the height of six feet six, weighing two-hundred forty pounds. The wrestling coach said, "Why don't you be on our team?" That skinny little runt became a world renowned wrestler. Why? Because one day he faced his fear.

Fear torments - especially the fear of failure. I felt the agony of failure in 1987 while establishing Hillcrest Church. We experienced internal conflict. A serious power struggle ensued. No one won. The church suffered. There were many days when I wondered if the congregation would survive.

It did! After all, God birthed Hillcrest Church, not Morris Sheats or any other man. It is God's church. His hand has preserved it. Today, it is a dynamic, flourishing congregation full of love. Truly a place "Where love touches people."

The fear of failure, however, almost succeeded. Very few encouraged me to continue the church. "Give it a dignified burial," was the advice of many.

Yet - even in the darkest moments of deep defeat - God's Spirit caused me to believe that the fear of failure could be overcome. Slowly - ever so slowly God began to ignite the fire of hope. A plan emerged. God is good!

II. ASK GOD FOR A PLAN TO CONQUER YOUR FEAR.

A young man in college, about to graduate, came to me and said, "You know, I am afraid to date. I just cannot relate to the young ladies. I have a tremendous fear of them, and I am ashamed to ask any of them to go out with me." It was a very real problem. I said to that young man, "God wants to give you a plan." This truth really gets exciting. God wants to give you a plan of action to conquer your fear. God is FOR you. He wants you to conquer fear.

You see, it says in Exodus,

> *And the Lord said unto Moses, Wherefore criest thou unto me? Speak unto the children of Israel, that they go forward; but lift thou up thy rod, and stretch out thine hand over the sea, and divide it: and the children of Israel shall go on dry ground through the midst of the sea.*
>
> Exodus 14:15, 16

Notice carefully what this says. It was Moses who was crying out to God. When he was crying out to God, God gave him a plan. The people were afraid. I am sure there must have been some fear that gripped Moses' heart, too, but he said, "I am not going to be afraid. The Lord God has given me a plan." As I was counseling with the young man, I advised that he pray and ask God for a plan to approach a young lady that he was wanting to date. He said that he would, and as he began to pray and seek God, he told God about his fear of being rejected and asked God to give him a plan. Later, he asked me if I thought a particular idea would work. I said, "Do you believe it is from God?" The young man said, "I really do." Well, when I united that couple in marriage some time later, I realized God had given him the right plan, and he had used it to bring glory to God. They had a most holy wedding. As they stood there, the Spirit of God descended upon that place, I said, "Oh, God, I thank you for a young man who had the courage to face his fear and use the plan which You gave him." God does not want His people emaciated with fear. He wants us free and liberated so we can flow and move in a society that needs an answer for today. First, face your fear. Secondly, ask God for a plan of action to conquer your fear.

That is what a man did in a little place in Florida. He found himself with a piece of ground with just a bunch of scrubby trees and a lot of rattlesnakes, and he said, "What am I going to do?" He tried to get all the stumps and the trees out, but he was not successful. Trying to farm in that condition did not work. One day when he feared failure was inevitable, he said, "God, you gave me this land, what in the world do you want me to do with it? All I have is a bunch of rattlesnakes." The Lord gave him a plan. He began to learn about the rattlesnakes. He learned that he could extract venom from the snakes and help people in hospitals and clinics, when they had been snake bitten. He now has a marvelous business to the extent that each year twenty thousand people visit his farm, and the little town nearby is called Rattlesnake, Florida. God gave him a plan.

God has given some of you a plan, but you have let fear destroy that plan. You have said in your heart, "What can I do with it?" You are like the man who was left with money to invest. When the owner of the investment came back and said to the stockbroker, "What have you done with my investment?" he said, "l didn't do anything. I just held on to it, because I was afraid." The Bible says in that parable that the owner who left the investment with the man said, "You have been an unfaithful servant." Do not let fear paralyze you. God gives you a plan, and you see it. Then do what God has shown you.

As I have mentioned, internal conflict arose in the early years of the church I now pastor. In fact, the congregation decided to stop the building program. I will never forget the day we draped a wire fence around the concrete slab and $200,000 worth of steel. It was a funeral for many people. It was for me.

In the middle of the night, I would walk the land and pray, "Oh, God, raise up this steel. Finish what you have started." My wife would sit in the car and pray.

One day, a young architect in the church asked to see the building plans. He came back very excited and showed me a way to build the building at a much reduced amount of money, yet keep the initial design ideas intact. I knew God was up to something.

Some days later, a thought came to my mind. Two years had elapsed since the fence went up on the property. Our people were praying. Prayer services were held on the property. Communion was celebrated on the land. Faith was sown, where defeat had seemed triumphant.

"Go talk to the contractor" - the thought persisted. He is a good man. He listened. We shared ideas. He recalculated the job based on the ideas God gave the young architect. We were able, with God's help, to build phase one of our building.

III. YOU MUST BE WILLING TO WORK THE PLAN GOD GIVES YOU.

After you know what God has told you to do, you must get involved in it, and that is the third step. YOU MUST WORK THE PLAN GOD GIVES YOU. You have to start. Moses said, "We are going to go forward. We are going to execute the plan that God has given unto us, and I am going to be obedient to the plan." So they came to the Red Sea. God had told Moses, "Lift up your hand when you get to the Red Sea." He could have said, "I am not going to lift up my hands. Why, all those people will think I look silly sticking my hands out over that water." He could have said, "Not me, Lord, not me. Get Aaron. He likes to deal with water." But Moses was obedient to the plan God had given him.

If God has given you a plan and you have refused to execute that plan, then the reason why you are in the throes of despair and indecision is because you have not worked the plan that God has already given you. First, you face the fear; second, you ask God for the plan; and then third, you start working the plan that God gives you, and you will see those fears conquered. Work the plan. Start!

There are two problems in the world that are very large and affect almost everyone. The first one is that by far the majority of people in the world today do not have a plan for their life. The second problem is that if they do have a plan, they are sitting on it and doing nothing with it. I am saying to you, break loose from fear that has immobilized you. And say, "To God be the glory. I will work the plan that He has given me." START! Start this week; do not wait until another time.

When God begins to work in your life, be faithful to it. We should have no limitations as to what we can do - because God is able to raise us up. You say, "Well, that sounds like arrogance and egotism." It is just the opposite. It is a humility of falling upon the arms of our merciful Lord and Savior and saying, "I submit unto you. You give me the plan, and I will be faithful to it."

IV. YOU MUST BE WILLING TO FAIL.

YOU MUST BE WILLING TO FAIL. You say, "Boy, I do not like that idea." Moses had no written guarantee signed by God that when he raised his hands the waters would part. God had simply said, "I am going to do it." When God gives you a plan, there is an element of faith involved, and you must be willing to step out. Sometimes you do not even know if there is going to be a place for your foot to land. About the time you realize there is not a place, the Lord is going to slip a little dirt underneath. You see, God does not hold us responsible for success. God holds us responsible for obedience. There have been times God has told me to do things and, in my judgment, I have fallen flat on my face. You say, "Well, it must not have been God." Oh, yes, it was the Lord. However, there are times when His plan does not necessarily meet our definition of success.

In Jesus Christ there is a freedom to fail. You say, "Well, I do not know. That is kind of new. I never heard about that." Well, have you ever studied the early church? Talk about some failures. Those early Christians were so prejudiced, it took them years to realize that God loved someone other than just the national Jews. There is conflict in nineteen chapters in the Acts of the Apostles. The early Christians met lots of failures. They did, however, listen to God and kept working the plan of Acts 1:8.

"Do not tell me God can heal a Gentile." I can just hear some of the brethren discussing that over coffee. "You mean to tell me that God has gone outside of his chosen race? You mean God is moving on those people?" God gave Paul a plan and He worked it. Even when to some it appeared to be a mistake, Paul was willing to be obedient. By the power of the Holy Spirit, God raised that early Church, from a place of contention and fighting to a place of authority that rattled the cage of Caesar's empire.

V. KEEP WORKING THE PLAN.

God is going to give you a plan, keep working it. What is your fear? This week get alone with God and ask Him to give you a plan to conquer that fear and then work the plan. Do not give up. Moses did not stop. God said, "Moses, I am going to take these people to Canaan." And so, when the children of Israel kept on complaining and murmuring, fussing and fighting, he did not give up. He got angry sometimes, but he never stopped. He continued to lead. You say, "Well, he was disobedient, he did not get into Canaan." That's right! But the fact of the matter remains, he still worked the plan God had given him. Even when he was disobedient, he kept working God's plan.

God is not looking for perfect people, but obedient people. He wants us to mature. To grow. To be strong. However, God looks at maturity as a process. Most Christians view maturity as an event.

No! Maturity is a process of growth. Part of the process is continuing to be obedient even when you sin. Look at David. Paul. Peter. All sinners - yet all obedient to God's plan.

Reread Hebrews 11. After the great litany of "faith giants" is given, a little phrase leaps of the page in verse 34 - "whose weakness was fumed to strength". These were ordinary, sinful people. One was a prostitute. Another was a murderer. God used each person because they were obedient.

Keep working the plan. You know what will happen? God will change you into a new creation. He will take away the fear and give you life. A dear friend and his lovely wife come to mind here. Several years ago this couple came and visited with us. The sanctuary of the church I pastored at the time was under construction. My friend, who had been a minister for several years, had become somewhat disillusioned with all the things he saw wrong in the church. Many ministers have. He said, "Morris, I am going to a new town. I do not have anyone with me except my family, but God has given me a plan. God is going to give me an answer to my prayers to have a church where people from all backgrounds can come together and worship and praise the Lord." He shared some of his thoughts with me. He asked me questions about how our church was functioning and how things were going. At that time, we were experiencing some hardships. A few days later, he and his family moved to the new city.

Several days ago, when I was passing through that city, I stopped for a visit, and he took me over to a beautiful new sanctuary which seats about a thousand people. The people are coming and being healed and touched by God's Spirit. I will tell you why. Because a man asked God for a plan and then kept on working the plan God gave him. I want to encourage someone reading this to not give up. God gave you a plan long ago. Do not give up on it. Keep working the plan that God has given you and you are going to see results. Faith defeats fear!

Whatever your fear may be - it is not too big for God. Face your fear and ask God for a plan. Then work that plan to the glory of God. As He heals you of that fear, thank Him for the results and keep on working the plan.

CHAPTER 11

THE DANGER OF COMPARISON

For I say, through the grace given unto me, to every man that is among you, not to think of himself more highly than he ought to think; but to think soberly, according as God hath dealt to every man the measure of faith.

Romans 12:3

Sometime ago, many years ago in fact, I attended regularly what was known as a preachers' meeting. Ministers would meet each month supposedly to encourage one another; that was the idea. One of the reasons why I stopped going was - I never got encouraged. The first question was always, "How are things at your church this week?" Some of you know what that question means. If you do not, it means, "How many did you have in attendance last Sunday?" So, if you say, "Well, thank God, the Lord has really been blessing," they would say they were happy about that. But then they would finally get around to asking, "Well, how many did you have in attendance?" I always got the feeling that the whole thing was geared to a state of comparison, in which you had to achieve a little bit more each month to be accepted.

I counseled a person once who said to me, "I have a sister who can do everything better than I can." She went on to pour out her soul, how she felt in comparison to this sister. Another lady told me, "My husband simply does not have it." I wondered why she married him, because she was constantly comparing him with everyone else. She thought her husband just did not have what it took to be a success. So, over the years I have made an interesting study of, what I might call, THE DANGER OF COMPARISON. Satan slips in very unobtrusively and involves us in a very casual, nonchalant way of comparing ourselves with someone else.

It all seems harmless at first. It seems perfectly innocent for one preacher to ask another preacher, "How is your church. How many did you have in attendance? etc., etc." The result of comparing yourself, however, with other believers can often be devastating. It can often be one of the worst tricks that satan plays on you to cause you to think, "Well, I am not quite up to par." Or, "Look at me. I'm really doing great."

I. ACCEPT YOURSELF.

Look with me in I Corinthians 7:18-24.

> *For instance, a man who already has gone through the Jewish ceremony of circumcision before he became a Christian shouldn't worry about it; and if he hasn't been circumcised, he shouldn't do it now. For it doesn't make any difference at all whether a Christian has gone through this ceremony or not. But it makes a lot of difference whether he is pleasing God and keeping God's commandments. That is the important thing.*
>
> I Corinthians 7:18, 19 (Living Bible)

First of all, you must ACCEPT YOURSELF. It does not make any difference whether a Christian has gone through this ceremony or that ritual or joined this church or that church. It makes a lot of difference, however, whether he or she is pleasing God and keeping God's commandments. It goes onto say:

> *Usually a person should keep on with the work he was doing*

> *when God called him. Are you a slave? Don't let that worry you, but of course, if you get a chance to be free, take it. If the Lord calls you, and you are a slave, remember that Christ has set you free from the awful power of sin; and if he has called you and you are free, remember that you are now a slave of Christ. You have been bought and paid for by Christ, so you belong to him, be free now from all these earthly prides and fears. So, dear brothers, whatever situation a person is in when he becomes a Christian, let him stay there, for now the Lord is there to help him.*
>
> I Corinthians 7:20-24 (Living Bible)

This Scripture is basically saying that we have a role in life to play. It is the role of simply being what God wants us to be. We are not to try to be someone else. The moment you and I try to be like someone else is the moment we fall into the danger of comparison.

Let's look in I Corinthians 12. After this long discourse about the physical body, Paul compares it to the spiritual body. He says there are parts of the body that are not even seen, but all the parts of the body are important. He uses this to show how every member in Christ is important.

> *Now ye are the body of Christ, and members in particular. And God hath set some in the church, first apostles, secondarily prophets, thirdly teachers, after that miracles, then gifts of healing, helps, governments, diversities of tongues.*
>
> I Corinthians 12:27, 28

Surely somewhere in that verse you could find something you could do. Maybe you cannot do miracles. Well, I am not very good at that either. I wish I had a greater gift there. Maybe your gift is not speaking in tongues, but perhaps it is giving some kind of special help. Notice, there is a gift of helps. I do not see how anyone could get out of that one.

Whatever God has ordained for us to do, we must always allow different members of the body the freedom to function in the way that God plans for them. There will be spiritual activities from time to time about which you might think, "Well, that is not for me." If, however, it is for someone else, if it builds and strengthens the body overall, then that is the beautiful thing about the body of Christ. So be it. We do not have to compare ourselves. We can each find our own ministry and serve there.

> *Are all apostles? Are all prophets? Are all teachers? Are all workers of miracles? Have all the gifts of healing? Do all speak with tongues? Do all interpret? But covet earnestly the best gifts: and yet show I unto you a more excellent way. This is the way of love.*
>
> I Corinthians 12:29-31

In other words, we are not to compare ourselves to each other and say, "Now, let's see. You have the gift of teaching and you are really fantastic. I cannot teach effectively. I just have not been blessed with that gift. Poor me." You begin to run yourself down because you are not a teacher. The person, however, who is a teacher may be a lousy helper. Perhaps they cannot really help someone along the way of life like you can. Do you follow me? We must find our place in the Body and then minister from one motive and one motive alone: that is the motive of LOVE. I Corinthians 13 comes between chapters 12 and 14 for a reason. It is there because the whole message is, any gift that God gives to us should be used joyfully, in the spirit of love.

For example, what if the eye were to say, "Because I can see, I am the most important part of the body." And the eye would say to the little toe, "You are very insignificant down there. You just get dirty and stink and you just do not do anything. In fact, you are just in the way. You know, we could do just fine without you. I am the eye. I can see. I am giving all the light to this whole body. And there you are. Just a little ole thing stuck out there on the edge." Then some time in the middle of the night, when it is dark and the eye cannot see, you stump your little toe, and something up in the head says, "WOW.

That little toe is still down there, guiding the body when the eye cannot." What is the point? The point is this: the little toe needs to be down there and serves a purpose. Just as in the body of Christ there are those who speak or sing or teach; there also, must be those who can serve, love, and even take care of the place of worship.

I remember visiting a small town in Guatemala. A village named Juteapa. I was only nine or ten years of age.

For some reason, I do not know why, I noticed a beautiful bouquet of flowers in front of the pulpit. I asked the missionary about them.

He explained that a poor woman from the country brought them each week. "It was her gift of seeing," he told me. Then he added, "She walks nine miles, one way, with her six children to bring the flowers every Sunday morning." I have never forgotten that lady. Her gift was simple, yet beautiful.

I was reading this last week in the Old Testament in I and II Chronicles. The Levites were divided up into maintenance men, ushers, and musicians. And all that was considered unto God as a Holy and Divine work. When a person walks down the aisle of your church ushering, helping people in and out, I want you to know that is as much a ministry unto God as the man standing behind the pulpit preaching the sermon. We often do not look at it that way, but that is the way we should look at it because that is the way God looks at it.

The Bible tells us over in Galatians that Peter and Paul were sort of comparing notes. They were entirely different from one another. Peter was boisterous, loud, and impulsive. Paul was rather calculating and decisive. He thought things through very carefully. Galatians 2:7 has an interesting little passage.

> *But contrariwise, when they say that the gospel of the uncircumcision was committed unto me, as the gospel of the circumcision was unto Peter; (For he that wrought effectually in Peter to the apostleship of the circumcision, the same was mighty in*

> *me toward the Gentiles;) And when James, Cephas, and John who seemed to be pillars, perceived the grace that was given unto me, they gave to me and Barnabas the right hands of fellowship; that we should go unto the heathen, and they unto the circumcision.*
>
> Galatians 2:7-9

Here is the whole point of the story. Peter was called of God primarily to work with those of Jewish background. Paul was primarily called to work with those of non-Jewish background. If you will go on and read the entire passage, you will find that Paul and Peter did not always agree. Even when they did not agree, however, they realized that they each had a place in the body of Christ, and that is the way it should be. We do not have to agree on every single doctrinal and theological issue. But we must, beyond any shadow of a doubt, we must, give place to each other to function within the body of Christ. That is essential. I beg of you to understand what I am saying unto you. We all have different ministries, and we function in different ways. But oh, to sit around comparing ourselves with each other is not what God wants. He wants us, rather, to find our place in the body and then begin to act. Love always produces action.

Friction within a body of believers usually develops when someone wants to function where someone else is serving. I am sure that many of you have never had a problem like that, but a lot of people do. They say, "I do not know why she gets to sing. I mean, well, I can sing better." We begin comparing what we are doing with what someone else is doing, next we begin to get uneasy, and then we begin to get hard to get along with, and that is exactly what satan wants. He wants to create contention and confusion within the body of Christ. Comparing yourself to others is not good. It is not good at all.

Look with me further in Galatians.

> *For ye are all the children of God by faith in Christ Jesus. For as many of you as have been baptized into Christ have put on Christ. There is neither Jew nor Greek, there is neither bond nor*

free, there is neither male nor female:
{Black nor white not brown nor red nor yellow; rich nor poor, good suit on, no suit at all. I added a little bit there in that verse in case you were getting lost. It ends up by saying:}
For ye are all one in Christ Jesus.
Galatians 3:26-28

A lady said to me this week, "I visited your church just a Sunday or two ago, and I was deeply impressed by the love I sensed there. I was impressed to see that there were people of different races who were worshiping together; and no one seemed to be upset about it." That was exactly what spoke to her heart. I said, "Praise God, we are all one in Jesus Christ." We must realize that the glorious truth of the Gospel is that Jesus loves every single person. Jesus loves children! Jesus loves adults! Jesus loves teenagers! Jesus loves us: everyone!

> *For we dare not [now I want you to notice that terminology] We DARE NOT make ourselves of the number or compare ourselves with some that commend themselves: but they measuring themselves by themselves, and comparing themselves among themselves, are not wise.*
II Corinthians 10:12

Now, do not try to read that verse real fast. You will never make it. If you read it very slowly, you will see that we are not to measure ourselves by others. We are not to compare ourselves among each other. We DARE NOT do that.

> *But we will not boast of things without our measure, but according to the measure of the rule which God hath distributed to us, a measure to reach even unto you.*
II Corinthians 10:13

There are some things that are beyond my measure; there are some things that are beyond my ability. The first passage I gave you in this chapter said that to every man is given a measure of faith. There are some things that have been given to you, that have not been given to me, and vice versa. We are not to step beyond that which is measured unto us; when he said, "Unto you is dealt a measure of faith." To put it in 20th century language, Paul is saying every one of you has a certain ability, and you are to use that ability for God. That means that everyone reading this is really an okay person in God's sight. You can function the way I cannot. But we blend and harmonize, and we compliment and supplement each other.

II. RESULT OF COMPARISON.

Now let me give you two RESULTS OF COMPARISON. When you begin comparing yourself to someone else, two things are inevitable. First, you can always find someone who is doing a better job than you are. So, if you compare yourself to him or her, then what is the result? You feel condemnation. Can anyone show me a place in the Bible where it says that God wants you to be beat down with condemnation? No. It says just the opposite.

> *There is therefore now no condemnation to those which are in Christ Jesus, who walk not after the flesh, but after the Spirit.*
> Romans 8:1

The glorious truth is that you do not have to live under condemnation any longer. That is why I say that the danger of comparison is brought on by satan. He comes in and says, "Just look at the way so and so is doing that job, and look how you do it." You begin to compare yourself, next you begin to condemn yourself, and the next step in that process is anger.

In the Old Testament, I Samuel 18, there is a story about King Saul who sent out one of his young captains by the name of David. David had a marvelous victory against the Philistines, and as he was coming back, the ladies danced in the streets, and they said, "Glory to David. David is the man of the hour. Saul has slain his thousands, but David has slain his tens of thousands." And ole Saul had his upstairs window open listening to all this. The Bible says he was very "wroth," which means, "He was mad as he could be."

From that moment on, Saul determined he was going to destroy David. You can read the whole story in I Samuel 18, 19, and 20. He was determined to do everything he could to kill David. He humiliated him; instead of putting him over thousands of men, he gave him only one thousand men to supervise. You know what was wrong with Saul? He was comparing himself with David. If he had been a real man of God he would have been saying, "Oh, thank you God, that you have sent unto me this young captain to help me protect Israel."

Secondly, you can always find someone who is not doing as well as you are, and comparing yourself with them produces pride. You see, it works both ways. You can be proud because you are doing so much better than they are doing. What does the Bible say about pride? (Incidentally, this verse is the middle verse in the entire Bible. Isn't it interesting which verse comes right in the middle of the entire Bible?)

> *Pride goeth before destruction, and an haughty spirit before a fall.*
>
> Proverbs 16:18

When you think you have arrived, you had better watch out because you are headed for trouble. Pride goes before destruction. You can always compare yourself to someone with whom you are doing better, and then you have pride.

In Acts 12, Herod Agrippa gave a speech which was so eloquent and filled with oratorical ability that the people said: "It is god. It is god who is speaking to us." Herod Agrippa said,

That is right. It is god speaking to you." The next verse says he died and the worms ate him up. That is pretty simple, pretty straightforward; just as it says in Proverbs, "Pride goes before destruction." Herod Agrippa learned the hard way. I would like to spare you that kind of lesson.

What is the solution; if I am not to compare myself to others who are doing better; if I am not to compare myself to someone who is doing worse, what am I to do? You are to accept your place in the body of Christ and be happy as to the person you are. Let's read Romans 12:3 again.

> *For I say through the grace given unto me, to every man that is among you, not to think of himself more highly than he ought to think; but to think soberly, according as God hath dealt to every man the measure of faith.*
>
> Romans 12:3

It does not say we are to run ourselves down. It says we are to think seriously according as God hath dealt to every man the measure of faith. You are to evaluate your abilities. Now, I do not want you to misunderstand. There is nothing wrong with knowing that you can do a certain job and you can do it well. It is not egotistical to be aware of your capabilities. Egotism is when you tell everyone what a great job you can do, whether you really can or not. So do not finish this chapter and say, "I am not supposed to say, I have a certain talent." Yes, we are to know which talents God has given us so we can use them, but we dare not start comparing ourselves with one another. Each of us has a place in life and in the body that we must fulfill. Once we find that place, let us minister with contentment, and let us praise the Lord.

The psalmist David said,

> *Let the words of my mouth and the meditation of my heart be acceptable in thy sight.*
>
> Psalm 19:14

Wouldn't you rather be accepted in God's sight than in someone else's? If you know that you are doing what God wants you to do, then you can be happy with yourself and stop fighting this battle of comparison.

CHAPTER 12

CAUSES OF DEPRESSION

I will bless the Lord at all times: his praise shall continually be in my mouth. My soul shall make her boast in the Lord: the humble shall hear thereof, and be glad, O magnify the Lord with me, and let us exalt his name together. I sought the Lord, and he heard me, and delivered me from all my fears.

Psalm 34:1-4

I have chosen as a basis for some of the things I am going to share with you a book entitled *None of These Diseases* by W. I. McMillan, M. D. I would encourage you to read it, if you find it. In reading this book, and I have read it many, many times, there is a favorite story of mine about a couple who comes to see Dr. McMillan and explains that they are unable to sleep. The fact that insomnia has set in is especially disturbing to them because they have always been able to sleep well. After examination, Dr. McMillan finds there is no apparent physical illness to cause their problem. It seems that everything is in order. As they come to the end of the medical interview, the lady takes a letter from her purse. She says, "I know this sounds strange, but I wonder if this letter could have anything to do with our problem? It was written to my husband by a neighbor." This is how the letter went.

Dear George,

I understand that you are selling some eggs to Harry Bickerstand. You people should know that I have invested considerable money in the chicken business and I am able to supply more eggs to the people in this little hamlet than they are able to eat. You ought to know that my business is hurting by your dabbling around with a few hens and selling eggs to Harry. I think that you ought to stop.

Your Neighbors, Mattie and Casper

Then she said, "Doctor, we have a right to sell eggs. Casper's eggs are white. Harry Bickerstand prefers our brown eggs, and we ought to be able to sell him a few eggs; but ever since we got that letter we cannot sleep." Then she said, "Do you think we should get out of the egg business?" A few weeks later the daughter of the couple came by to see the doctor and said, "Guess what my folks did?" He said, "Well, I wonder. What did they do?" "They got out of the egg business." You see, they found that it was a whole lot cheaper, because the doctor bills were costing more than they were making selling a few eggs to Harry Bickerstand.

Now, we chuckle and say, "Well, they had a right to sell eggs." But if they were being upset by a letter from a neighbor about the eggs, then they did the smart thing by getting out of the egg business. You say, "Do you really believe that? Are you telling us that every time something happens causing a discord inside us, we should change?" That is exactly what I am saying! Life is simply too short for us to have broken relationships that result in a state of depression. Because of a situation with a neighbor who acted unreasonably, a couple was forced to sacrifice their rest and health.

Now, I would like to discuss with you some of the causes of depression. I call these The Classical Causes. Basically, they are very simple; there is nothing profound about them, but toward the end I intend to give you something which I believe is a new thought from the Lord.

I. DISAPPOINTMENT

The first classical cause of depression is what we might call DISAPPOINTMENT, just plain old disappointment. A man came to me many months ago and said, "You know, I was scheduled to receive a promotion in my company, but I was passed by. It was very disappointing." "In fact," he said, "I have been terribly depressed over the whole thing." I understood what that man was saying. A disappointment had come his way and he was depressed. I have counseled literally thousands of people, and so many times they have said, "I feel depressed." Why? They had been disappointed. Something was not going right in their life. Or maybe nothing is even wrong, but circumstances are not what you had imagined they would be, and you are disappointed.

For example, there is the young mother who experiences what the doctor calls post-partum depression. After that lovely baby is born into the world, the mother may go into a tremendous state of depression. After all the months of looking forward to this one day - the birth of her child - she now realizes that the big event is over and instead of having a little cuddly bundle of love that is the epitome of baby food commercials, always has a "pampered" bottom, and smells like the essence of talcum, all of a sudden the real truth comes crashing in. The little darling is red and wrinkled, is wet all the time and smells bad. What that new mother is going through is the disillusionment of her fantasies. This does not happen to every woman, but it happens to many. Is it abnormal? Not necessarily; it is a part of life.

Perhaps you were disappointed in school. You were expecting an "A" and you got a "B." Oh, that hurts. And a little depression sets in. Why? Because you are disappointed.

What is the correct pattern we should have when dealing with depression that is caused by disappointment? Everyone reading this

127

will be disappointed sooner or later, if it has not happened to you already. How are you going to handle it? I believe the Christian response to disappointment should be determination. You say, "How can I have determination?" Let me share with you a most remarkable passage.

> *Of the Jews five times received I forty stripes save one. Thrice times was I beaten with rods, once was I stoned, thirce times I suffered shipwreck, a night and a day I have been in the deep: In journeyings often, in perilsof waters, in perils of robbers, in perils by mine own countrymen, by the heathen, in the city, in the wilderness, in the sea, among false brethren; {perils everywhere} in weariness and painfulness in watching often in hunger and thirst, in fastings often, in cold and nakedness.*
> II Corinthians 11:24

You know, that is a pretty bad report. Do you get depressed reading that passage? I am just glad that I was not Paul. He was always getting into trouble for the Gospel's sake. He wanted to go to Spain. He dreamed of preaching the Gospel at the furthest point of the Western Empire, which was Spain, but instead he ended up in prison. A hole in the ground, where it is wet with a little tiny opening at the top to get in, and where you are handed your food. He could have said, "I give up. What is the use? I am defeated; I am disappointed. I am disgusted. I quit." But instead he said,

> *Therefore, I take pleasure in infirmitie, in reproaches, in necessities, in persecutions, in distresses for Christ's sake: for when I am weak, then am I strong.*
> II Corinthians 12:10

Would you read aloud that last phrase? "For when I am weak, then am I strong." When I feel weak in my abilities, when I feel like there is no hope, when I feel extremely disappointed, then I turn to God and say, "Within myself I cannot handle the load." Then the Holy Spirit comes upon me and gives me the determination I need. When you are down; when you are defeated; when you are disappointed;

when depression sets in; get alone and count the cost. If you are willing to go all the way with God, then realize that He will not put more on you than you can handle. The Bible teaches that. I Corinthians 10:12 says that we will not be tested with more than we can handle. Read it!

II. UNFAIR COMPARISON

Another classical cause of depression is what I call UNFAIR COMPARISON. In his book *How to Win Over Depression*, Dr. Tim LaHaye says, "Most of the time we match an area of our deficiency against someone else's strength." What a word of wisdom. "Well, I just can't sing like she sings." Okay, maybe she can't bake a cake like you can. The devil delights when you compare yourself against someone else. He loves it. Because we know that when you begin to compare yourself against others, you will not compare strength to strength, you compare weakness to strength and that leaves you weaker. You feel washed out, you feel self-pity; you feel depressed.

> *For we dare not make ourselves of the number, or compare ourselves with some that commend themselves: but they measureing themselves by themselves, and comparing themselves among themselves, are not wise.*
> II Corinthians 10:12

You say "What in the world does that mean?" Very simply it says this. When you compare yourself with other people, you are very unwise. Perhaps you go to a class reunion. Everyone there is assessing one another so fast, you can almost hear the wheels clicking. You say, "I wonder how he got that position. He sure was not that smart!" Or, "You know, he is so ugly, how in the world did he get her? She really is good looking." Or, "I am pretty good looking. I wonder if I made a good choice?" Then someone tells you their kid made the varsity football team, and yours did not even make the Junior varsity.

Here we go starting a whole new cycle of depression for the next generation. Let me tell you one simple way to ruin a kid real quick. Continually compare him to someone else and point out his weaknesses. That is a fast way to crush a kid. "Why can't you play the piano like Susan plays the piano?" The little kid says inside, "Mom and Dad think Susan is better than I am."

Unfair comparison. The problem is that we are programmed from the time we are little tiny toddlers to rate ourselves on a scale against everyone else. The child comes home with his first report card, and the parent looks at it and says, "Not bad. How did the other children do?" Never ask that question. Your kid is not everyone else. He is just himself/herself.

All anyone can do is the best they can do. If you are a "B" intellect, do not frustrate yourself because you are not an "A" intellect. But if you are an "A" intellect, and you are lazy and make "B's" because that is what the majority of the "other" kids make, then pray through. Get with it! Do the very best you are capable of with the talent God has given you. That is true success - doing the best you can with the gifts God has given you.

Here is a new definition for success. Success is simple well-being under God. It has nothing to do with houses or cars or bank accounts. It has everything to do with whether or not you feel well and you like yourself and if you have a sense of well-being. Then you are a successful person.

III. REJECTION

A third classical cause for depression is REJECTION. Rejection! Let me tell you a story. Some time ago I was called to a home occupied by an older person. This person said, "Pastor Sheats, I have asked you to come because I watch you on television. My health is bad and I cannot attend the services." This person, late in life, somewhere in their eighties, began to unfold a story that ripped my spirit to shreds. I have never been touched more by any account of a life. The person told me, "You know when I was a young teenager my parents did not want me. They arranged for me to get married. They shoved me out. The man I married did not love me, and as soon as I became pregnant, he did not want me either. There I was with a baby and no one wanted me." This dear lady began to unravel a whole series of episodes that absolutely would make any novel appear to be boring. It was the most unbelievable string of rejections that I ever heard in my entire life. And finally this person ended her story by saying, "I guess I can summarize it all by saying that for 85 years I have felt like nobody wanted me alive!"

Can you imagine the depression, the gloom, the total dejection in that house? But even in the midst of the heartbreaking despair, there was an answer. Just as the answer for disappointment is determination, and the answer for unfair comparison is to be happy with who you are in God, so the answer for rejection is to realize that God has never rejected anyone.

As I took those wrinkled hands into my hands, I began to pray. God began the healing of her memories. I shared with this lovely elderly lady how she could be healed. As the Power of God descended upon me, I prayed with the anointing of the Spirit of God. Through prayer we walked back through the corridors of time until we felt the hand of the Holy Spirit healing her of the scars of a teenager being kicked out of her home; healing her when she became a mother far too young, healing her of the scars of the years when she was left to care for her family without help. The power of God not only restored her life, He gave her something she had never known before: unconditional love. I thought when I left there, "Hallelujah, Jesus, you said it, 'Come unto me, all you who are weary and heaven laden and I will give you rest.'"

Of course there are many other classical causes of depression: the loss of something or someone dear, traumatic change, or chemical imbalance in the body. Fortunately, our medical doctors are learning a great deal about how improper body metabolism can cause depression, and many people are finding help today just through the proper kind of diet.

Now I come to what I consider to be two rather new ideas that I have not read in a book, but for several years God has been teaching me. I do not claim that they are some great revelation. I do feel that this is something new, at least, to my spirit.

IV. IMPROPER SPEECH

The first one is this. Many times we have depression because of IMPROPER SPEECH. "Improper speech," you say. "What do you mean by that?"

> *Where no wood is, there the fire goeth out: so where there is no talebearer, {no gossiper} the strife ceaseth. As coals are to burning coals, and wood to fire; so is a contentious man to kindle strife The words of a talebearer {the words of a gossip, the words of one who speaks evil} are as wounds, and they go down to the innermost part of the belly.*
>
> Proverbs 26:20-22

Now, I ask you a question. What goes down to the innermost part of the belly? The words of the gossip, the talebearer. I said, "God, what does that mean?" Because you see we have had a lot of sermons preached on, "If you speak evil of someone else, you are cutting them down, you are destroying them." But the Lord said to me, "In addition to hurting another, the critical issue here is when we speak evil of others we are also cutting ourselves apart, and the wounds go down to the pit of the stomach."

What happens to you when you have a broken relationship with someone? What happens to you when you speak evil to someone or of someone? Your stomach begins to tie up in knots. Dr. McMillan lists all kinds of things that people have from just getting angry: ulcers, arthritis, heart problems, and many more. We know that when you bear false witness against anyone, when you speak evil of them, when you cut them asunder, they are not going to be hurt half as badly as you are going to get hurt. Your words are as wounds going down to the most inner part of your being and you are going to feel it. You are going to feel that old stomach tying up. You will have no peace, and you will be frustrated. You say, "That is pretty tough." It really is. What we say with our mouth is very much related to our physical well being.

There is a Scripture in Ephesians 4:29 which I would like to ask you to memorize. It begins like this, "Let no corrupt communication proceed out of your mouth." Then "Let none of it come out but that which is good to the use of edifying." What is edifying? Building up. Finally, "That it may minister." Minister what? "Grace unto the hearer." Now read it all aloud.

> *Let no corrupt communication proceed out of your mouth, but that which is good to the use of edifying, that it may minister grace unto the hearers.*
>
> Ephesians 4:29

Now, what really makes you feel good? You are going along, you meet someone you know, and he says, "You are all right. I am for you. I love you. I thank God for you. You are my buddy, and I want you to know that I believe the best in you." That makes you feel good and makes you stand up a little bit on the inside. Right? But what if someone else comes along and says, "You know, I think if you wore your hair another way it would look better on you, and did you know you really should have worn a different tie with that suit?" As they are slashing you apart you are saying, "Oh, thank you! You really made my day!" No. People cut you asunder, and you do not like it.

Every once in a while, we will have a strange phone call - someone who is really taking us to task about something with which they disagree. I learned a long time ago you just have to say, "Thanks for calling. I appreciate your interest." You have to learn to bite your tongue. Though you may want to tear what they have said apart, it will not solve a thing. You see, when you become angry, it releases adrenalin in your body and that adrenalin travels all through your body and your blood pressure goes - ZOOM. Some of you know what I am talking about. And what makes us feel that way? Improper speech. The Scripture goes on to say in Ephesians,

> *Let all bitterness, and wrath, and anger, and clamor, and evil speaking, be put away from you with all malice.*
>
> Ephesians 4:31

Get rid of anger and bitterness. If you have anything inside you that is making you bitter, do not finish the day without making it right. The Bible tells us in Hebrews chapter 12 that a root of bitterness will spring up and will defile everyone who is nearby. There is no place for bitterness or anger in the Kingdom of God. But, oh, how we cop-out. We say, "Well, I just can't help it. I get mad, and I just can't help it." Someone is angry with you at the office. You go home and you kick the dog. Then you open the door and your little kid says, "Daddy. Daddy." And you say, "@!!*. leave me alone," and they take off. You do not have to be angry at life. God really does want the best for you, and anger destroys your ability to handle the issues of life. Guard your words carefully.

V. UNREALISTIC GOALS

Finally, many people have depression because not only do they use improper speech, but they have UNREALISTIC GOALS. Many people have goals that are too high. Perhaps they had an ambitious mother or father who pushed them too hard. They could never succeed because the goal was so high they could never reach it. On the other hand, some people are lazy, and their goal is not high enough. They never try, so they never achieve anything, and they are not happy. A lazy person is never happy.

We must have a properly balanced goal. Now how can we find that? I will tell you how. By evaluating the gifts God has given you and being content with the way He has made you. That principle is spelled out in Romans.

> *For I say, through the grace given unto me, to every man that is among you, not to think of himself more highly than he ought to think.*
>
> Romans 12:3

We are cautioned not to over rate ourselves. Well, how should we think about ourselves then? We should consider the way God has made us, not think more highly of ourselves than we are. We must find our niche in life, do the best we can with our abilities, and then be content with who we are. Some people are never content. No matter how much they succeed, or how many accomplishments they make, they are never content. Do you know why? They have unrealistic goals. You must reach the place of understanding your capabilities as well as your liabilities. A balanced, mature person will evaluate his strength and his weakness. He will not focus on his weakness. He will focus on his strength, but he will keep an adequate goal before himself and God.

I encounter people all the time who are frustrated because they have unrealistic goals. Many do not become apparent until one reaches his or her fifties or sixties, when all of a sudden they realize, "Man, I am 13 years away from retirement." They begin to think that they must do everything overnight. People have heart attacks, and they fall by the wayside because they have, or have had in the past, unrealistic goals. We must find our pace and position in God and steadily move along toward that which God has for us to accomplish. You will find that you will be a much happier person.

Allow me to finish this chapter with a paragraph from Dr. William Saddler, one of America's foremost psychiatrists. I am assuming that he must have been a Christian, or he probably would not have written these words. This is what he writes:

No one can appreciate as fully as a doctor the amazingly large percentage of disease and suffering which is directly traceable to worry, fear, conflict, immorality and ignorance, to unwholesome thinking, and unclean living. With sincere acceptance of the principles and teachings of Christ, with respect to the life of mental peace and mental joy, the life of unselfish thought and clean living would at once wipe out more than half the difficulties, disease and sorrows of the human race.

Dr. Saddler simply states that if people would apply the teachings of Jesus Christ to their lives, we would wipe out immediately - IMMEDIATELY - one-half of the difficulties, diseases, and sorrows of the world. I suggest it is time that we start taking the teachings of Jesus seriously.

When He said, "Take no thought for tomorrow. Tomorrow shall take care of itself," He was saying, "Under my eternal Father, I will live one day at a time." That is the way to conquer depression. My secretary said to me a few days ago, "How do you cope with everything that happens to you in one day?" I said to her, "Because it is the only day I have and with His help I can make it one day at a time." Borrow not from tomorrow for tomorrow will take care of itself. This afternoon there was a fleeting moment in which my schedule for tomorrow ran through my mind. As quickly as it ran through, I let it run right on out, because tomorrow is not here yet. The Spirit of Jesus is within me, living one minute, one second at a time.

This is a divine principle that I would pray to God that every one of you would learn. Through the power of Christ, you can learn how to conquer depression and live a successful life with a sense of total well-being. Because when Christ comes in, He brings confidence to face tomorrow.

CHAPTER 13

HOW TO RECEIVE THE GREATEST BENEFIT FROM YOUR PROBLEMS

We all have problems, so I think it is time we learned how to receive the most benefits from them. Most of us desire to have quick solutions to our problems, but that is not necessarily the will of God. Sometimes God is trying to establish what we should call "character development" through our problems. If we do not learn the lesson God is trying to teach us the first time, He will probably let you take the test over. He wants all of His children to be good students. If you fail to see what God is trying to say to you through a problem and what area of your character He is trying to develop, then it may be that you will have that problem again. Let us consider some benefits from our problems.

I. YOU EXPERIENCE GOD'S GRACE.

The first important benefit from our problems is that we receive more GRACE FROM GOD. Now the word "grace" is a derivative from the word "charis" and it speaks of a gift. God wants to give us the gift of strength, the gift of power, and the gift of favor.

For it is God which worketh in you both to will and to do of His good pleasure.

Philippians 2:13

God is trying to work out His will and good pleasure in every one of our lives. You say, "How in the world could my problems be the development of God's good pleasure?" Because God sees you the way you can become, rather than the way you are. See! Jesus looked at Peter, and He saw before Him "the shiftless one," but He saw further down the road, that he, Peter, would become "the rock." Many times in the Bible, a person's name is changed because God does not look at them the way they are. He looks at them the way they can become! That is why Jesus changed Peter's name from "Cephas" to "Petras."

When we have problems, God is trying to give us more grace, more strength and more power to endure and to develop our character. After all if Christianity is not just a "Blessing Club," the Christian must be willing to have developed within him strong, mature character so that when the difficult times of life come, it is the Christians who stand the most authoritatively in the world and say, "There is an answer." The rest of the world will say, "We want to know what it is." IT is the grace of God working through the problems in your life. What does James 4:6 have to say?

> *But He giveth more grace. Wherefore He saith, God resisteth the proud, but giveth grace unto the humble.*

James 4:6

God gives more grace. God resists the proud but gives grace unto the humble. Now one thing God is looking for in our lives is a humble and a contrite heart.

> *…Yet I will look with pity on the man who has a humble and a contrite heart, who trembles at my word.*

Isaiah 66:2 (Living Bible)

What is a contrite heart? The "heart" is another word for the "will" of a person. Thus a humble and contrite "will" is when you are willing to let God work out His plan in your life rather than trying to work out YOUR plan in your own life.

Now I did not say a broken spirit. You see, you do not want to break a child's spirit, but you do want to break his will. The scripture tells us,

> *A merry heart doeth good like a medicine: but a broken spirit drieth the bones.*
>
> Proverbs 17:22

If a child has a rebellious will, however, under the authority of God that will must be broken, in order that God might deal with his inner spirit. That is why we, as parents, must have an abundance of delicate wisdom in knowing how to minister to our children.

The "heart" or "will" of a person is their basic attitude, their basic flow, their basic outlook. Our basic outlook should be one of humility and one of knowing that God is over us, and we ourselves are only that which God allows us to become. That is a beautiful example of a broken and a contrite heart.

If you have never been broken, if you have never had your world torn apart, sooner or later chances are, God will allow your world to be shaken so that out of brokenness a more mature spirit will be born. It was not until Mary broke the alabaster box, not until it was cracked open did the ointment and sweet smell come forth. It is not until we are broken of our pride that God is then free to flow out of us. God cannot use a proud man or woman who is arrogant and says, "Look at me." God cannot use that kind of man or woman because they have already become their own god. God will not use a person who is their own god. He alone is God. He will not be second place to anyone or anything, anywhere at any point in time. He will be number one and that is all.

God is saying to us through our problems, "I want to give you more grace to become the kind of person I want you to become." Nothing is more humbling than experiencing conflicts which we cannot solve, and then having to turn to God. Many a man has found God when he ran into a conflict that he was unable to solve.

Out on my dark days of conflict and sorrow, God spoke to me. I bumped into God. He spoke clearly to my mind.

"You have spent too much time on your secondary gift of ruling, I cannot bless you. Spend time on your primary gift of preaching/teaching, and I will give you great favor."

My life changed. Out of "the eater came forth sweetness." Out of what seemingly would destroy me, came extra grace to be broken and hear God's voice clearly. What a blessing!

II. JUDGE YOURSELF

The second benefit from your problem is the benefit of JUDGING YOURSELF.

> *For if we would judge ourselves, we should not be judged. But when we are judged, we are chastened of the Lord, that we should not be condemned with the world.*
>
> I Corinthians 11:31, 32

Here we are taught to examine ourselves to see what is inside. Notice verse 28, "For let a man examine himself." Now, this passage is talking about taking the Holy Communion, but when we come to our problems, we can examine ourselves and say, "Lord, what is it that you are trying to say unto me?"

> *For whom the Lord loveth He chasteneth, and scourgeth every son whom He receiveth.*
>
> Hebrews 12:6

The word "scourge" is really the idea of correction. Because He loves us, He wants to correct us and discipline us. When we have a problem we should begin to ask ourselves, "What is it that God is trying to correct in my heart?" I would like to give you another passage that confirms this:

> *For the commandment is a lamp; and the law is light; and reproofs of instruction are the way of life.*
>
> Proverbs 6:23

When we are reproved or corrected, it is because God is trying to bring out in us a better way of life.

I have experienced a much better way of life since 1988. On that sabbatical, God spoke to my heart. He literally changed my priorities.

God forced me to examine myself. Through the process God strongly impressed my inner man that I was spending too much time on administration of the local church and not enough time on preparation to preach and teach. "More time must be spent in prayer and preparation" - was the message. The clarity of the Word was so strong that I changed my weekly schedule rather drastically.

Over five years have elapsed, and it is definitely a better way of life. God's way always is the better way.

III. GOD'S WORD COMES ALIVE

A third benefit is the benefit of GOD'S WORD COMING ALIVE. How many times have you been in the Word of God because a problem drove you to the Word? You were searching to find an answer. You were trying to find direction.

> *Turn you at my reproof: behold, I will pour out my spirit unto you, I will make known my words unto you.*
>
> Proverbs 1:23

When God corrects us, we do some turning, and then what happens? God will pour out His Spirit upon us, and He will do what? He will make His Word known unto us. Some of the most meaningful understanding of the Word of God in my life has come through the most difficult hours of my life. When I was suffering deep inside because of the anxieties of the moment and the problems that faced me, the Lord would give a Word which would bring tremendous power and insight and glory. We must not go back on the Lord when we face a problem. Let us stand strong and say, "God, you are trying to teach me something. You are trying to give me new wisdom, new insight, new authority. I thank you for it."

When we face a problem and we gain new Biblical insight, that is just one more area where satan cannot defeat us. That is exciting. It is exciting to know that we can have Biblical insights, which we can stand upon in the hour of crisis. Every man has a Waterloo, and when you face your Waterloo experience, when you face your defeat experience, when you face the time when you do not know where to go, that is when God by His Spirit is trying to drive you into the Word so you can be filled with new power.

What did Jesus rely upon when He was being tempted? The very worst time in the early outset of His ministry, when He was being tempted severely, He did what? He stood on the Word of God. He would say to satan, "Thus says the Lord God. It is written." Satan cannot handle that. Let me give you some thoughtful ideas when you are experiencing difficult times. Let me suggest you remember Psalm 119:71.

It is good for me that I have been afflicted; that I might learn thy statutes.

That is pretty strong. Sometimes when we are afflicted, we are learning the statutes of God. I have learned that one of the things to do when you are going through a difficult time and you are trying to gain Biblical insight is to read the Psalms and mark every sentence that sort of "leaps out" at you.

Secondly, study the Proverbs. One chapter per day will take you through one month, and then you can begin over.

Thirdly, read a good spiritual biography. Recently, I was going through a difficult time, and I began to read again the life of David. As I read the life of David, the shepherd and the king, it brought tremendous insight and new guidance. I was able to stand strong in the hour of real testing, because of a spiritual biography of a man who lived thousands of years ago.

By the way, for your own personal library, I would urge you to invest a few dollars periodically in spiritual biographies of contemporary people like William Carey, Hudson Taylor, Kathyrn Kuhlman, Mother Teresa, Robert Morrison, and others. You can go to the book store and just ask for the Christian biographical section and begin to read the Word of God through the lives of outstanding men and women of God.

IV. FAMILY UNITY

The fourth benefit that comes from our problems many times is the benefit of FAMILY UNITY. Many times a family is unified through a problem they have been unable to solve. If there is a problem you are facing and you cannot solve it as a family, you should call a family get-together. Ask everyone to meet in the living room or den, and the head of the family should say: "Now, what is causing this problem? What has happened to our family? What have we done wrong?" Often when a teenager becomes rebellious and nasty toward the parents, the parent amplifies the problem by defending their parental position. Many times God is trying to speak to the parent through the teenager's rebelliousness. Many times God is trying to say to the parent, "You have missed the mark. You have not been sacrificing your time in prayer. You have not been spending time in the Word of God with your family, and now you have a rebellion in your own household." Many times God is trying to say to the head of the household, "If you will humble yourself before God, I will heal your house."

A man said to me a few days ago, "I knew we had a terrible problem; our whole family was falling apart. I called the family together, admitted that I, as the head of the house, was really out of the will of God. It brought my family to their knees, they began to pray for me, and we became more unified than we have ever been before." If your prayers are being unanswered in your household, there are several reasons why.

V. DISCOVERING WHY OUR PRAYERS ARE NOT ANSWERED

Now I am going to give you ten reasons WHY YOUR PRAYERS ARE POSSIBLY UNANSWERED. I am just going to state them and let the Spirit of God deal with you about them, because I know that God has a reason when our prayers are unanswered, and many times it is something within us.

1. Iniquity

> *If I regard iniquity in my heart, the Lord will not hear me.*
> Psalm 66:18

You must not have iniquity in your heart. What is iniquity? Iniquity is leaning toward sin. It is not altogether the overt action of the sin, but it is just that leaning toward sin. The heart is not right.

2. Condemnation

> *For if our heart condemn us, God is greater than our heart, and knoweth all things. Beloved, if our heart condemn us not, then have we confidence toward God. And whatsoever we ask, we receive of Him, because we keep His commandments, and do those things that are pleasing in His sight.*
> I John 3:20-22

God does not want his children living under condemnation, and I John 3:20-22 tells us when we do, our prayers will be hindered. If you sense any kind of condemnation, ask God to heal your heart.

3. Occult Mind

> *Any Israeli who presents his child to be burned to death as a sacrifice to heathen gods, must be killed. No Israeli may practice black magic, or call on the evil spirits for aid, or be a fortune teller, or be a serpent charmer, medium, or wizard, or call forth the spirits of the dead. Anyone doing these things is an object of horror and disgust to the Lord, and it is because the nations do these things that the Lord your God will displace them. You must walk blamelessly before the Lord your God.*
>
> Deuteronomy 18:10-13 (Living Bible)

God is very concerned about our minds. He says in Deuteronomy 18:10-13 that we are not to be involved in any kind of activity that would seek direction from any other source. So many people are missing the mark here. They do not understand the seriousness of the advances satan is making on our society today. We need to be so sensitive in this area that we would not allow anything of occult origin to touch our families. Horoscopes, palm reading, ouija boards, and many games which appear to be innocent must carefully be avoided.

In addition to this, the number one place we have to be careful is the television, because more and more television is becoming harmful to our minds. Recently, we turned on the TV to watch something together as a family, and it had not been on fifteen seconds until one of my adult children said, "We cannot watch that." The very starting scene was something to do with satan worship and the occult. Thank God for discernment.

4. Refusing the Truth

> *He that turneth away his ear from hearing the law, even his prayer shall be abomination.*
>
> Proverbs 28:9

If you refuse the truth, your prayers will not be answered. Truth is penetrating. Truth, however, sets us free. The process of hearing the truth, accepting the truth, and acting on the truth is a major challenge. Truth ignored, on the other hand, hinders the effective answering of our prayers.

5. Pride

If my people, which are called by my name shall humble themselves and pray...then will I...heal their land.

II Chronicles 7:14

Pride is so difficult to discern in our own personal lives. I am not always aware of my pride. It takes a deep sensitivity to the Holy Spirit to maintain a sincere heart free from pride.

Pride is one of seven things that God calls an abomination - something to be abhorred. Pride must be kept in check.

Self-worth is proper, however. We are strong because of Christ Jesus who lives within us. He gives us confidence. Self-worth is understanding that every person has value. Pride is believing that I am worthy because of my position in life. Self-worth is based on the favor of God. Pride is based on things.

6. Wrong Motives

Ye ask, and receive not, because ye ask amiss, that ye may consume it upon your lusts.

James 4:3

If your motives are wrong, your prayers are not going to be answered. It is not wrong to pray that God will bless your business, but if you are praying that God will bless your business so you can become a millionaire and have power to control people, you have got the wrong motive.

7. Dishonoring Your Companion

Likewise, ye husbands, dwell with them according to knowledge giving honour unto the wife, as unto the weaker vessel and as being heirs together of the grace of life; that your prayers be not hindered.

I Peter 3:7

In I Peter 3:7 God is talking to the man and God expects the man to put his wife and companion in a place of respect and honor. If the husband does not honor his wife, his prayers are going to be unanswered or they are going to be hindered. This goal can be difficult. If a wife is rebellious and unsupportive, a man finds great difficulty in honoring and respecting her. However, it can be done. The husband can learn that his trust is in God. His hope is in God. Therefore as an act of sacrificial worship, a husband can honor and respect his wife - even if she is a difficult person.

8. Unforgiveness

For if ye forgive men their trespasses, your heavenly Father will also forgive you; But if ye forgive not men their trespasses, neither will your Father forgive your trespasses

Matthew 6:14, 15

If you have an unforgiving spirit, your prayers will not be answered. Forgiveness is not an option. We must practice forgiveness. It is an act of the will - to forgive.

9. Doubt

If any of you lack wisdom, let him ask of God, that giveth to all men liberally, and upbraideth not; and it shall be given him. But let him ask in faith, nothing wavering. For he that wavereth

> *is like a wave of the sea driven with the wind and tossed. For let not that man think that he shall receive anything of the Lord. A double minded man is unstable in all his way.*
>
> James 1:5-8

When doubt comes in, your prayers are hindered. Learn to verbalize to God your doubts. The more specific the better. Confessed doubt can be turned into faith through the power of prayer.

10. Unbelief

> *Then came the disciples to Jesus apart, and said, Why could not we cast him out? And Jesus said unto them, Because of your unbelief: for verily I say unto you, If ye have faith as a grain of mustard seed, ye shall say unto this mountain, Remove hence to yonder place: and it shall remove; and nothing shall be impossible unto you.*
>
> Matthew 17:19-20

Unbelief, of course, is a great hindrance to all of our prayers. Doubt is a question raised in the mind. Unbelief is a conclusion that says, "I do not believe." Doubt and unbelief are different.

God wants us to pray for each other that we may be healed, that our families may be strong. I do not believe that we have any problem that comes our way, except God intends for us to benefit in some way. It may not be in all five of these areas, but it will be in some of them. I pray that we will begin to take our problems as a glorious blessing from God, who is the solution to every need. As a friend of mine said after the loss in death of his nine year old daughter, "I do not trust God because I understand. I trust God because there is much I do not understand."

AFTERWORD

KEEPING YOUR EMOTIONAL HEALING

This book of the law shall not depart out of thy mouth; but thou shalt meditate therein day and night, that thou mayest observe to do according to all that is written therein: for then thou shalt make thy way prosperous, and then thou shalt have good success.

Joshua 1:8

This remarkable passage gives us the real secret for KEEPING YOUR EMOTIONAL HEALING. It is important to realize that God wants you continually, emotionally whole. You can maintain emotional wholeness by following the guidelines in this verse. Let us consider these guidelines carefully.

I. SPEAK

First, "This book of the law shall not depart out of thy mouth." God is speaking to Joshua, the new leader of the children of Israel. Joshua realized the tremendous responsibility in leading the Israelites. Moses is dead. Joshua is the new leader. He feels the heaviness of responsibility upon his shoulders. At that time God gave him a Word. God said, "Joshua, remember to keep My Words in your mouth."

This meant that Joshua was to constantly speak forth the Words of

God. This is a simple pattern that you and I can follow today. When you keep God's Words in your mouth, life comes forth to your entire personality. My advice is that you actually read God's Word out loud daily.

II. MEDITATE

Second, the instruction from God came from Joshua to "meditate therein day and night…" Not only do you need to keep God's Word in your mouth, or speak it, but you need to meditate upon that Word. The word "meditation" in some circles has come to be a misunderstood word. There is so much being said today about different forms of meditation that people are confused. Is meditation good or bad?

I would like to suggest that meditation is very good if the content of your meditation is the Word of God. The problem with most meditation is that the content leads to no fruitful results within the mind of the person meditating. The person may become relaxed but they have not improved their mind. However, in meditating on God's Word not only do you experience relaxation, but you are helped in your thinking processes. Your mind becomes sharper and clearer even as you get older. Why? Because God's Word is powerful and renews the mind.

III. ACT

Third, the instruction comes to Joshua to "observe to do according to all that is written therein…" In other words a process is now developing. God said to Joshua - "Speak My Words. Meditate upon My Words. Do what they say!" Do you get the progression? It is a powerful process. Speak. Meditate. Act.

I have talked to many people in my life who wanted to do what God said but seemingly did not have the will to do so. What was their problem? I believe the problem is that many people fail to see the divine order in this process. When you speak God's Word out loud and meditate upon God's Word, then you will find it much easier to do what the Word of God says. The process is important.

A casual reading of God's Word oftentimes does not change the inner will. The Words must be meditated upon (sometimes I meditate upon one verse for six weeks). Then the will can be changed to do what the verse says. It is important to follow the steps outlined in God's divine process. I urge you to follow it carefully.

IV. SUCCESS

Fourth, God gives us the result when we follow the preceding three steps. "For then thou shalt make thy way prosperous, and then thou shalt have good success." Now I want you to go back and read the previous sentence again. Let me ask you, who is going to make your way prosperous and successful? For years I read this verse and thought that God would make me successful and prosperous, if I would do what the verse instructed. That is not what the verse says. The instruction from God is that the individual who does the first three steps, will then make his own way prosperous and successful.

Recently, I was meditating upon this verse and praying about the meaning. The insight came that prosperity and success should really be defined as "total well being." Now if you define those terms in that way, then the result is a complete personality, or wholeness.

How does a person come to find prosperity and success or "total well-being?" I believe the answer is in making right decisions. Right decisions or good judgments will only be made when the first three steps outlined in Joshua 1:8 are followed.

Here is the formula: You...

Keep God's Word in your mouth.

Meditate upon God's Word day and night. Do what God's Word says.

The Result...

You have prosperity and good success by making the right decisions.

I can personally say that I am experiencing wholeness (a continual process) by following the pattern outlined in Joshua 1:8. I have shared this with hundreds of people and have seen their lives changed by following this pattern. It would be useless to write an entire book about emotional healing and not tell people how to keep it. I hope that you will take these thoughts and read them over many, many times - until they become a part of your inner spirit. If you will do that, you will be emotionally whole. The good news that the entire world needs to hear is that YOU CAN BE EMOTIONALLY HEALED.